WISDOM
IN
SUFFERING

"Suffering touches every human–even those who really love and trust Jesus. My friend and colleague, Dan Burrus, has written an excellent book that I think can best be understood as a layman's guide to understanding suffering biblically. Dan brings his theological insights, thorough research, and his pastoral understanding of the width and depth of human suffering together to answer many of the questions believers have when they 'enter the valley of the shadow of death.' But more than just equipping our minds to understand a complex subject, the reader will be equipped to respond to suffering with joyous worship and steadfast hope for better days to come."

–Rev. Chuck McArthur
Executive Director
Equipping Leaders International

"Every generation must wrestle with the problem of pain: Why does it exist? From where did it come? Will it ever be conquered? In this concise little volume, inspired by the book of Job, Dan Burrus wrestles with these questions and many more. Here readers will find a rich theology of suffering, replete with relatable stories and wise pastoral counsel. Take it up, read it carefully, and grow in your wisdom and wonder."

–Brandon Crawford, PhD
Lead Pastor
Grace Baptist Church, Marshall, MI

"Scripture never tells us how Job acquired his wealth and large family; but it tells us a lot about why he lost them and how he, and others, responded when he did. As Daniel Burrus shows us in this excellent new book, the patience of Job needs to be understood in terms of God's purpose in his suffering (James 5:11)–and how that pattern of suffering relates to the work of Jesus Christ and the experience of all those who take up their cross and follow Him."

–Crawford Gribben, PhD
Professor of History
Queen's University Belfast

"Many Christians who are facing suffering are eager to receive healing balm for their soul through the wisdom of Scripture. Dan has written an important book with practical lessons Christians can glean from Job—a book that is really all about suffering. It will bless anyone either going through suffering themselves or desiring to help those in a dark and difficult season."

–Greg Salazar, PhD
PCA Pastor and Church Planter
Charlotte, NC

"It is fitting that one who has committed himself to teaching God's Word to others would serve us so well by writing a devotional commentary on the book of Job. For it is here that we readers join with Job in God's classroom of suffering as this divinely inspired story teaches us wise lessons on this all-too-familiar reality in our human experience. I love how Dan Burrus has taken a complex piece of wisdom literature and blessed us with clear interpretation, wisdom lessons drawn from that interpretation, and faithful application of those lessons for our lives. I heartily commend this volume to all believers who desire to know God more fully by learning of His Divine Providence through the wise lessons He teaches us in the school of suffering."

–Jon Pratt, PhD

Academic Dean and Professor of NT

Central Baptist Theological Seminary

Plymouth, MN

"Suffering is one of the great challenges that Christians face. Using Job as a lens to discuss suffering, Dan offers some helpful reflections on how a believer especially might glorify God in suffering. Job knew suffering, and Dan weaves Job's story into a narrative that allows him to encourage us in how to view and respond to our suffering. We will suffer in this world. Read this book and be encouraged in your journey."

–Jeff Straub, PhD

Professor of Historical Theology, retired

"Helping saints through suffering is the heart of Christian ministry. Pastor Dan's approach to the book of Job as wisdom literature for practical lessons on suffering is spot on. His exposition is crystal clear, written with helpful illustrations and real-life application. Dan writes with a well-balanced approach to the book of Job with solid theology, practical teaching, and a gospel trajectory in each chapter. I highly recommend this book!"

–Jeff Rich

Senior Pastor

Grace Community Bible Church

Lakeville, MN

WISDOM
IN
SUFFERING

LESSONS FROM
JOB

DANIEL W. BURRUS

AMBASSADOR INTERNATIONAL
GREENVILLE, SOUTH CAROLINA & BELFAST, NORTHERN IRELAND

www.ambassador-international.com

WISDOM IN SUFFERING: LESSONS FROM JOB
©2025 by Daniel W. Burrus
All rights reserved

ISBN: 978-1-64960-891-8, hardcover
ISBN: 978-1-64960-527-6, paperback
eISBN: 978-1-64960-568-9

Cover Design and interior typesetting by Karen Slayne
Edited by Sydney Witbeck

Titles may be purchased in bulk for education, business, fundraising, or sales promotional use. For information, please email sales@ emeraldhouse.com.

AMBASSADOR INTERNATIONAL
Emerald House
411 University Ridge, Suite B14
Greenville, SC 29601
United States
www.ambassador-international.com

AMBASSADOR BOOKS
The Mount
2 Woodstock Link
Belfast, BT6 8DD
Northern Ireland, United Kingdom
www.ambassadormedia.co.uk

The colophon is a trademark of Ambassador, a Christian publishing company.

*To the brothers and sisters in Sierra Leone, who know suffering
at an entirely different level.*

*To Grace Community Bible Church, who graciously received this
book first in sermon form.*

*And to my parents, especially my dad, whose interest in the book
of Job renewed my desire to study this biblical book.*

CONTENTS

Preface   1

Acknowledgments   3

CHAPTER 1
The Believer and Suffering   5

CHAPTER 2
Sovereignty and Suffering   15

CHAPTER 3
Satan and Suffering   27

CHAPTER 4
Emotions and Suffering   37

CHAPTER 5
Sin and Suffering   49

CHAPTER 6
Counsel and Suffering   59

CHAPTER 7
Wisdom and Suffering   71

CHAPTER 8

Justification and Suffering   83

CHAPTER 9

Justice and Suffering   95

CHAPTER 10

God and Suffering   107

CHAPTER 11

Evil and Suffering   119

CHAPTER 12

The Gospel and Suffering   129

Appendix   141

Bibliography   145

About the Author   149

Index   151

PREFACE

THE BIBLICAL BOOK OF JOB is difficult to understand for many Christians. And rightly so—we are thousands of years removed from the context and events that shaped the people in the story. Yet God has seen fit to preserve this ancient text for us.

Because God has given us the book of Job, Christians can profit from this book. Therefore, since God has preserved it for us and since all Scripture is profitable (2 Tim. 3:16), we must be able to learn from the book of Job.

Benefiting from the book of Job means capturing the main themes. Undoubtedly, suffering is a major theme in the book. Like the book of Proverbs, Job is written to give the readers wisdom. I believe, therefore, that God wants us to profit from the book by learning wisdom for suffering. Wisdom lessons abound in the book of Job as we trace the topic of suffering throughout the chapters. My humble attempt is to simply make these wisdom lessons more understandable to the reader of the book of Job, but this is not my ultimate aim.

Job is one book of many in Scripture. The Bible has more to say about suffering than what is contained in these chapters,

1

but the book of Job says much. Whether it is your own personal suffering, suffering in the ones you love, or suffering on a much larger, global scale, may God use these wisdom lessons in your life not only to attain wisdom in suffering but also ultimately to lead you to the Wisdom of God—Jesus Christ. The pursuit of wisdom, a pursuit from the dawn of time, is not an end but a means to an end of knowing, loving, and serving the Triune God. At the end of wisdom, you will find God. For truly "the fear of the Lord, that is wisdom" (Job 28:28).

Soli Deo Gloria,
Daniel W. Burrus

ACKNOWLEDGMENTS

IT'S CLICHE TO SAY A book is not written by one person. I owe many thanks to many people for this book.

First, I want to thank the brothers and sisters in Sierra Leone. For the last nine years, I have labored in Sierra Leone to teach church leaders to observe all that Jesus commanded (Matt. 28:20). While I have taught *them*; they have taught *me*—especially about suffering. These dear saints were constantly in my mind when writing this book.

Christians live in communities that gather regularly. Though I have been physically relocated to a new community, Grace Community Bible Church in Lakeville, Minnesota first heard and received the essence of these chapters in sermon form. They offered much encouragement and feedback along the way, including the nudge for me to put these messages to print.

Writing a book not only takes a community of people; it takes a lifetime. Hundreds of thousands of life experiences, opportunities, and trials enter every book that is published. With this, I thank my parents, particularly my dad, who expressed deep interest in the book of Job, therefore renewing my interest to study the book in greater depth. In addition, I am grateful for my wife and four children, who supported me in this entire process.

I also want to thank the team at Ambassador International, especially for giving a first-time author the opportunity to publish. The team has been invaluable along the way.

CHAPTER 1
THE BELIEVER AND SUFFERING

JOB 1:1–22

THE PURITAN JOSEPH CARYL SPENT twenty-five years preaching the book of Job. Maybe Caryl was trying make his congregation feel the message of suffering through twenty-five years in the book of Job.[1] When I preached through the book of Job, though I would have liked to expand on it as long as Caryl did, I limited my messages to one year. The congregation at Grace Community Bible Church had enough suffering of their own without me adding to it by preaching through Job for twenty-five years!

The book of Job, in large measure, is about suffering. It is not *ultimately* or *only* about suffering, but that is a main theme. Job is classified as wisdom literature. There is much wisdom we can glean about suffering from the book.

To start, there are three lessons we can glean from the first chapter about the believer and suffering.

---

1   Joel R. Beeke and Randall J. Pederson, *Meet the Puritans* (Grand Rapids: RHB, 2006), 135.

LESSON 1: SUFFERING HAPPENS TO
ALL PEOPLE, EVEN BELIEVERS

One of the great mysteries and complexities the book of Job explores is that suffering came to Job, of all people. Why is this so mysterious and complex? Job was godly, and he was great.

First, Job was godly; he was a believer. The book presents him this way: "There was a man in the land of Uz whose name was Job; and that man was blameless, upright, fearing God and turning away from evil" (Job 1:1). Job was, in fact, so godly that he offered continual sacrifices in case his children sinned. "When the days of feasting had completed their cycle, Job would send and consecrate [his children], rising up early in the morning and offering burnt offerings according to the number of them all; for Job said, 'Perhaps my sons have sinned and cursed God in their hearts.' Thus Job did continually" (Job 1:5). And even though he suffered greatly, Job 1:22 notes that Job did not sin or blame God for his suffering.

Though we do not know who the narrator of Job was, he was intent on saying Job was a godly believer. The author never questions Job's godliness. He is never cast as an unbeliever; the narrator never questions Job's faith. Job was also a model believer. He was respected—a leader, the guy everyone wanted to be like and be with.

But Job was also great. The opening verses describe this for us. "Seven sons and three daughters were born to him. His possessions also were 7,000 sheep, 3,000 camels, 500 yoke of oxen, 500 female donkeys, and very many servants; and that man was the greatest of all the men of the east" (Job 1:2-3). Job was a very wealthy man. And yet the irony and shock of the book of Job is that, of all people, suffering came to Job. Job was the least to deserve the suffering. We're meant to see that Job *shouldn't* have suffered, yet he did. That is what the author wants us to see. Job, a godly and great believer, suffered.

Suffering does not discriminate based on wealth, religion, language, ethnicity, geography, culture, or any earthly category. Suffering comes to all humanity. Suffering, to put it differently, is everywhere, universal, and unavoidable. We only need to look at 2020 to recognize that suffering comes to all. COVID-19 changed all our lives—believers and unbelievers. Suffering, like COVID-19, is truly a pandemic.

This means that those professing Christians and the worldviews that teach that suffering is a mirage, that suffering isn't real, that suffering doesn't exist, and that it's just a state of mind are flat-out wrong. Ask Job if suffering is real! The "happy, clappy, paste-a-smile-on-your-face" kind of Christianity isn't real! Believers suffer—truly suffer—and it is real! And those who want to say that if you have more faith or are godlier, suffering won't come to you or—when it does—you deserve less of it are wrong. Job was godly. He had great faith, and yet he suffered severely. Suffering comes to all people, even the godliest believers we know.

LESSON 2: SUFFERING ARRIVES
UNEXPECTEDLY AND FAST

There is nothing Job could have done to expect the suffering that came to him. Notice how the opening chapter delineates the timing of Job's suffering. Job 1:13-19 says:

> Now on the day when his sons and his daughters were eating and drinking wine in their oldest brother's house, a messenger came to Job and said, "The oxen were plowing and the donkeys feeding beside them, and the Sabeans attacked and took them. They also slew the servants with the edge of the sword, and I alone have escaped to tell you." While he was still speaking, another also came and said, "The fire of God fell from heaven and burned up the sheep and the servants and consumed them, and I alone have escaped to tell you." While he was still speaking, another also came and said, "The Chaldeans formed three bands and made a raid on the camels and took them and slew the servants with the edge of the sword, and I alone have escaped to tell you." While he was still speaking, another also came and said, "Your sons and your daughters were eating and drinking wine in their oldest brother's house, and behold, a great wind came from across the wilderness and struck the four corners of the house, and it fell on the young people and they died, and I alone have escaped to tell you."

I want you to notice something that we tend to forget as readers of Job's story—Job is not privy to the heavenly discussion between God and Satan in Job 1:6-12 and Job 2:1-6. Job was minding his own business, caring for his family; and out of the blue, suffering strikes. God did not warn Job, "Heads up, Job, a freight train is about to hit your life!" There was no warning whatsoever.

The time to prepare for suffering is now. Are you ready for suffering to strike? It's going to happen unexpectedly. Though you cannot prepare for suffering with absolute perfection, preparing does help. It's like the fire drills you used to have in school. Preparation helps.

Furthermore, the reality is we all are currently suffering to one degree or another, some in big ways like cancer and others in small ways like a canker sore. But when suffering comes in its full force, we must be prepared. The book of Job helps us get ready. It helps us know how to respond.

Not only does suffering happen unexpectedly, but it also happens quickly. Notice Job 1:14-15 again: "[A] messenger came to Job and said, 'The oxen were plowing and the donkeys feeding beside them, and the Sabeans attacked and took them. They also slew the servants with the edge of the sword, and I alone have escaped to tell you.'" And after three months, the events of Job 1:16 transpire . . . no! It was while the first messenger was still speaking, another also came . . . and Job lost the sheep and the servants. And then while he was speaking, Job lost the camels. And while that messenger was still speaking . . . Job lost his children. Bam. Bam. Bam. When it rains, it pours.

Something similar happened to me a few years ago though obviously not on the same scale. I remember vividly standing in the emergency room waiting in disbelief of what was transpiring. I was literally numb to the reality of what was happening to me. I was in shock, and I couldn't do anything to stop my appendix from bursting any minute. At one point, I was on the bed, about to be wheeled to the operating room; and the pain, for a moment, went away.

I told the nurse, "The pain is gone. Get me out of here!"

Very calmly, she said, "You're not getting out of it that fast!"

As fast as it came, I wanted to get out of it. But I couldn't stop appendicitis.

We live in a fast-paced world. We plan down to the second. I leave very little room for margin. I am expected to be at work on time, and I expect my flight to be on time. This is our expectation. This is how we live. If the bus is ten minutes late, people throw a fit. It is only when we have brief reminders of the fragility of life that we remember that life can fall apart in an instant. Health, wealth, and loved ones can be taken away in the blink of an eye, just as they were for Job. Why do we have to be reminded of this fact? The book of Job is a reality check that suffering comes unexpectedly and fast.

LESSON 3: SUFFERING IS AN OPPORTUNITY FOR YOU TO TRUST GOD

One of the things we're meant to see in this book is that suffering comes to Job as a believer. He was given no explanation of why suffering came. In fact, a large part of the book is taken up with everyone trying to give their explanation of *why* Job suffers. He searches for answers. His friends give him their answers. No answer is forthcoming.

This is so common. In suffering, everyone wants to know why. Why is this happening? Why me? Why now? But often suffering comes, and we don't have the reason why. We're not meant to always know why we suffer. If we know why suffering comes, we might be tempted to put our trust in an explanation rather than a Person. Suffering is meant to turn our hearts to God, even when we can't see a reason why the suffering is happening. In other words, suffering, for the believer, is meant to be an act of worship.

This reality hit home for me when a friend died from cancer in his early forties. I had the opportunity to get to know Chris. He was a minister at a sister church. In the last few years of his life, the cancer started to spread, causing his suffering to become more intense. During this time, he once said to me something I will never forget. It has changed my perspective on suffering. He told me, "Dan, God has given me the ministry of suffering." For Chris, suffering was an act of worship. It was an opportunity for him to trust and serve God.

This is exactly what Job recognized. Notice Job 1:20-21: "Then Job arose and tore his robe and shaved his head, and he fell to the ground and *worshipped*. He said, 'Naked I came from my mother's womb, and naked I shall return there. The LORD gave and the LORD has taken away. Blessed be the name of the LORD'" (emphasis added). What's Job doing here? He's trusting. He's worshipping. This is Job's response, and it should be ours.

Suffering takes from you. We see clearly what suffering took from Job—everything but his life (Job 1:21). But Job could worship the Lord even amongst all the loss and pain. Job did not find his identity, value, and worth in his wealth, success, career, family, or relationships. Because when all these blessings were taken from him, he could still say, deep down in his heart, "Blessed be the name of the LORD" (Job 1:21).

Suffering reveals what is truly inside of you. Suffering is like the hot water for the tea bag. When you put a tea bag in hot water, the hot water draws out what's inside. So it is with suffering. When you and I lose the possessions, relationships, or jobs we use to define our value and worth, our heart is exposed. We can put on a show of godly Christianity; but when suffering comes, it exposes what we are placing our hope and trust in. Suffering reveals what you value and cherish. What suffering are you experiencing right now? What do you not have that you long for? What have you lost—children, relationships, health, your job, your reputation? What is it that you feel you cannot live without?

However, the beauty of the gospel is that as a believer, you can worship the Lord, not *because* of your suffering but *through* it. Whatever suffering you are experiencing right now, don't waste your pain. Your suffering is a ministry. Your suffering can be an act of worship to the Lord. Your suffering is an opportunity to trust God, and that's what He longs for from you.

CONCLUSION

Suffering comes to all people, even believers. Even though it may come unexpectedly and quickly, suffering is an opportunity for you to trust God. These three lessons give us much wisdom for a life of suffering. But the book of Job answers so many more questions, like:

- Why do good people suffer?
- Why does God allow suffering, especially if He is good?
- How should I respond to others who are suffering?
- What role does Satan play in suffering?
- What role does sin play in suffering?

These are a few of the many questions with which the book of Job wrestles. It is to answer these questions that we will turn in the next chapters.

CHAPTER 2

SOVEREIGNTY AND SUFFERING

JOB 1:1-2:13

HISTORICAL DRAMA FILMS HAVE ALWAYS captivated me. Drama films are my way to live in the shoes of another. Most Hollywood drama films, however, do not include one major character in their dramas: God. This is the essence of the secular worldview. The secular worldview is that life works without God. More specifically, the secular view says that because suffering exists in the world, there could not be a God Who is good, wise, just, and powerful. Suffering is merely chance, coincidence, or fate; or at best, if God does exist, He is cruel—not good, just, and wise.[2]

The secular worldview is at odds with the Bible—specifically, the book of Job. The "drama film" of Job presents an all-powerful God Who is also good, just, and wise. Unlike Hollywood films, this is what makes the book of Job one of the best historical dramas ever.

---

2   Timothy Keller, *Walking with God through Pain and Suffering* (New York: Penguin, 2013), 271. Kindle.

SOVEREIGNTY AND JOB'S SUFFERING

When you read the first two chapters of the book of Job, a question arises: who or what is responsible for the suffering Job experienced? The answer is nuanced. There are many "things" responsible for Job's suffering: people, nature, Satan, and God Himself.

First, people are responsible for the suffering—even people with evil, malicious intent. "[And] the Sabeans attacked and took [the oxen and donkeys]" (Job 1:15a). Then another group of people, the Chaldeans, destroy Job's livestock and servants. "While he was still speaking, another also came and said, 'The Chaldeans formed three bands and made a raid on the camels and took them and slew the servants with the edge of the sword, and I alone have escaped to tell you'" (Job 1:17).

Second, suffering not only comes from people but also nature. In Job 1:16, we read about lightning: "While he was still speaking, another also came and said, 'The fire of God [a way of speaking about lightning] fell from heaven and burned up the sheep and the servants and consumed them, and I alone have escaped to tell you.'" And in verses eighteen and nineteen, a huge windstorm—perhaps a tornado—killed Job's children: "While he was still speaking, another also came and said, 'Your sons and your daughters were eating and drinking wine in their oldest brother's house, and behold, a great wind came from across the wilderness and struck the four concerns of the house, and it fell on the young people and they died, and I alone have escaped to tell you.'"

In addition, not only people and nature, but Satan himself inflicted suffering on Job. Satan is also responsible. "Then Satan went out from the presence of the LORD and smote Job with sore boils from the sole of his foot to the crown of his head" (Job 2:7).

Finally, though people, nature, and Satan are responsible, God is ultimately responsible. It was God Who *initiated* the conversation with Satan in the first place. "The LORD said to Satan, 'From where do you come?'" (Job 1:7a). God began the conversation with Satan. Furthermore, God invited the conversation about suffering. "The LORD said to Satan, 'Have you considered My servant Job? For there is no one like him on the earth, a blameless and upright man, fearing God and turning away from evil'" (Job 1:8). Even in Job 2:2, in the second round of suffering, the Lord takes initiative: "The LORD said to Satan, 'Where have you come from?'" Then in Job 2:3, "The LORD said to Satan, 'Have you considered My servant Job?'"

Not only does God initiate the suffering with Job, but God permits it to be carried out. Notice that Satan must seek permission from God to harm Job. "Then the LORD said to Satan, 'Behold, all that [Job] has is in your power, only do not put forth your hand on him.' So Satan departed from the presence of the LORD" (Job 1:12). Again, in Job 2:6, Satan asks God permission to hurt Job personally; God gives him permission. "So the LORD said to Satan, 'Behold, he is in your power, only spare his life.'" The point is that since God initiated the conversation with Satan and permitted Satan to harm Job, God is the One ultimately in control, not Satan. Martin Luther famously said, "Satan is God's Satan."

Even Job himself recognized that God was responsible for his suffering. Job said in Job 2:10: "But [Job] said to [his wife], 'You speak as one of the foolish women speaks. Shall we indeed accept good from God and not accept adversity?'" It is clear that in all this Job did not sin with his lips. Certainly, Scripture would *not* say that Job did not sin with his lips if what he said about God being ultimately responsible for his suffering was not true.

For an even clearer example, perhaps we should look at Job 1:21, "[Job] said, 'Naked I came from my mother's womb, And naked I shall return there. The LORD gave and the LORD has taken away. Blessed be the name of the LORD.'" It doesn't say, "Satan has taken away." And notice what it says about Job in verse twenty-two: "Through all this Job did not sin nor did he blame God." The passage would not say this if what Job said about God bringing on suffering was sinful. Timothy Keller summarizes this well. He says, "The book of Job does not depict God Himself inflicting all these things on Job. This is a brilliant way to get across the truth that, while nothing happens outside of God's plan, God does not will evil things like He wills the good. God is not out of control of history, yet He does not enjoy seeing people suffer."[3]

In summary, many "things" are responsible for Job's suffering, but God is ultimately in control of what took place in Job's life.

---

3   Keller, 275.

YOUR SUFFERING AND GOD'S SOVEREIGNTY

Here is the wisdom lesson from these first two chapters about sovereignty and suffering that we can glean: God is Sovereign over all the suffering in your life. It is not right to say God is in charge of all the good things that happen in your life, but He is not in charge of the bad things that happen.[4] Yes, God uses secondary causes—like people, nature, Satan, or even your own decisions for good or ill—to bring on His Sovereign will for suffering.

But I want you to be rock solid! You need to be able to take this to the bank; you must be able to die on this hill. It must be firmly settled in your mind that *all* suffering you personally have experienced, are experiencing, and will experience or all the suffering you walk through with loved ones and friends is from God's Fatherly hand. Here are only a few examples of the kinds of suffering anyone can face:

cancer	abandonment	car accidents
mental illness	job loss	stroke
tooth pain	allergies	broken bones
spousal hostility to Christianity	financial struggle and pressures	singleness but wanting to be married

---

4   Paul David Tripp, *Instruments in the Redeemer's Hands: People in Need of Change Helping People in Need of Change* (Phillipsburg: P&R, 2002), 143.

- an unequally yoked marriage
- wayward son or daughter
- divorce
- hip pain
- aging parents
- estranged father

- Multiple Sclerosis
- barrenness of the womb
- skin rash
- a broken toy
- chronic pain
- handicapped child

- single parenting
- chronic infections
- infidelity
- job pressures
- loneliness
- Alzheimer's disease

- death of a mother, father, son, son-in-law, loved one, or friend

Your suffering is not the product of randomness or the forces of evil triumphing over the forces of good. I use each of these words deliberately. Think about it. Doesn't it seem a bit "random" that all of Job's suffering came upon him the same day—at least, all the first round. Why did the lightning "just so happen" to fall on the sheep and servants? How is it that a great wind "just so happened" to hit the house his children were in?[5] It's not randomness or chance; it's God.

There are forces of good and evil, as it were. But these forces are not independent or inanimate, like "the force" in Star Wars. The first two chapters of Job make clear that these forces—God

---

5   Vern Poythress, *Chance and the Sovereignty of God: A God-Centered Approach to Probability and Random Events* (Wheaton: Crossway, 2014), 42.

and Satan—are not equal forces. God's power is absolute and supreme. Satan's power is secondary and subject to God's.

God is absolutely Sovereign over all the suffering in your life; there are no random events, and there aren't any "forces of evil" triumphing over the "forces of good."

RESPONDING TO YOUR SUFFERING

The question is what should you do with this truth? What does it do for you knowing that God is Sovereign over all the suffering in your life? What is your response? What was Job's? Job clearly recognized that God was the ultimate cause of his suffering. Yet the Scriptures also pronounce that Job "did not sin with his lips" (Job 2:10).

So how do you hold this tension together? How do you reconcile the fact that Job saw God as ultimately responsible, but he did not "blame God?" There is an answer to this question, but there is also tension that you must live with which cannot be completely sorted out in this life.

The word "blame" could be translated "charge with wrong."[6] We could say that Job did not "charge God with wrong." In other words, Job did *not* say that God had an evil intent. Job did *not* say that God did anything wrong to him, and this demonstrates his trust and worship in God in the middle of suffering. Yes, Job

---

6   Francis I. Andersen, *Job: Tyndale Old Testament Commentaries* (Downers Grove: IVP, 1976), 93.

questioned. Yes, Job wrestled. Yes, Job did not see clearly. But he still trusted!

OBSTACLES IN YOUR SUFFERING

But trusting God amid pain, loss, and suffering is not easy. We struggle just as Job struggled. He wasn't perfect. There are several reasons why we struggle to trust.

Suffering causes us to lose perspective. We become overwhelmed and think, *I have it worse than Job*, or *They don't really understand what I'm going through.* I'm not suggesting we compare our suffering to Job to alleviate suffering we experience. The book of Job does not call you to *minimize* your suffering, but it never says we must be stoic about it. The point is that when you suffer, you tend to focus on yourself, not God. It's what happens. Job is written to teach you and me wisdom in our suffering. We can recognize God is Sovereign; and thus, we have a real-life opportunity to trust Him. The book gives us perspective. Read the book of Job when you're suffering to gain perspective.

If your suffering clearly comes from someone else or a natural disaster, it is easier to trust God. For example, if a tornado blows down your house, it can be easier to trust God because you had no control over it. But if the suffering is self-inflicted, it is harder to trust God—for example, if you failed to stop at the stop sign and become paralyzed or if you made poor financial decisions and have to file for bankruptcy. In these examples, you might be tempted to emphasis your responsibility to the detriment of recognizing God is Sovereign. But does God use other people and natural disasters to bring on suffering but not use you? God is Sovereign over your sins and poor decisions, even when they might bring on suffering.

You may want answers and want to know why suffering is coming upon you. But the book of Job teaches us that it is not ultimately necessary for you to know *why* you are suffering. It may be helpful, but it is not necessary to know the reasons. It is necessary, however, for you to know *Who* brought about your suffering. You need to trust that He is good, wise, powerful, and just. Suffering, according to Tullian Tchividjian, allows us to leave "the prison of How and Why" of suffering for "the freedom of Who."[7]

The wisdom we learn about God and His ways from these first few chapters is that God is Sovereign over all the suffering in your life. And this truth is made clear in the New Testament. Romans 8 is a chapter about suffering. "And we know that God causes all things to work together for good" (Rom. 8:28a). How could this not include our suffering? And therefore, since God causes all things—even suffering—it should cause us to remember the One Who suffered more than anyone else. "He who did not spare His own Son [from suffering], but delivered Him over for us all, how will He not also with Him freely give us all things" (Rom. 8:32)? Because God orchestrated the suffering

---

7   Tullian Tchividjian, *Glorious Ruin: How Suffering Sets You Free* (Colorado Springs: David Cook, 2012), 24. Kindle.

of Jesus—the greatest suffering known to man—how will God not give us all things that we need?

To put it differently, if God ultimately allows suffering in your life, He can certainly take it away. And if He doesn't take it away, even your suffering will not separate you from His love. Romans 8:35 says, "Who will separate us from the love of Christ? Will tribulation, or distress, or persecution, or famine, or nakedness, or peril, or sword?" All these forms of suffering do not separate us from His love. God caused suffering to happen to Job, but He never abandoned Job in the process, even though Job felt God had. Passages like Job 7:19 show this. And He will not abandon you in your suffering. Christianity "is not ultimately a defense from pain and suffering; rather, it is the message of God's rescue through pain [and suffering]."[8] So we trust Him just like the passengers on a plane trust their pilot.

When you're flying through big, puffy, white clouds on an airplane, you can't see anything out your window. Here's a news flash for you—neither can the pilots! But the pilots don't rely on their sight; they rely on and trust something else—the instrument panel. When the way is dark and we cannot see, we rely on and trust in the God Who made the way.

CONCLUSION

There are more questions you have. There are more questions that I have about the book of Job, but not everything can be

---

8   Tchividjian, 24.

dealt with in one chapter. The point is that God is Sovereign over all your suffering; and therefore, you can trust Him. Over two hundred years ago, two Christians beautifully illustrated this trust in God.

On September 24, 1754, the son-in-law of eighteenth-century pastor and theologian, Jonathan Edwards, died unexpectedly. Aaron Burr Sr. passed away just days before he was to be the first president of the College of New Jersey, now known as Princeton University. His wife, Jonathan Edwards' daughter, Esther, wrote this to a family friend:

> Your most kind letter of condolence gave me inexpressible delight, and at the same time set open afresh all the avenues of grief, and again probed the deep wound death has given me. My loss—shall I attempt to say how great my loss is— God only can know—and to him alone would I carry my complaint . . . had not God supported me by these two considerations; first, by showing the right He has to His own creatures, to dispose of them when and in what manner He pleases; and secondly, by enabling me to [someday] follow [my husband] beyond the grave, into the eternal world, and there to view him in unspeakable glory and happiness . . . I should not, long before this, have been sunk among the dead, and been covered with the clouds of the valley. God has wise ends in all that He does. [My husband's death] did not come

upon me by chance; and I rejoice that I am in the hand of such a God.[9]

Not less than eight months later, Jonathan Edwards died. Sara Edwards, Jonathan's wife, wrote this to Esther. Esther was the daughter who had just lost her husband eight months prior.

> My dear child, what shall I say? A holy and good God has covered us with a dark cloud. O that we may kiss the rod, and lay our hands on our mouths! The Lord has done it. He has made me adore His goodness, that we had him [Jonathan Edwards] so long. But my God lives; and He has my heart. O what a legacy my husband, and your father, has left us! We are all given to God; and there I am, and love to be.[10]

Esther and Sara understood and trusted in an all sovereign, wise, good, and just God, even amidst the suffering of loss. Whatever suffering you find yourself in, may you be able to say with them that "God has wise ends in all that He does"; and thus, "God has my heart," and "I love to be with Him."

---

9   Douglas Sean O'Donnell, *The Beginning and End of Wisdom: Preaching Christ from the First and Last Chapters of Proverbs, Ecclesiastes, and Job* (Wheaton: Crossway, 2011), 91-92.
10   O'Donnell, 91-92.

CHAPTER 3
SATAN AND SUFFERING

JOB 1:1–2:13

THE BOOK OF JOB IS a book about suffering. It is about more, to be sure, but not less. In the first chapter, we examined what the first chapter of the book of Job teaches about the believer and suffering. We saw three essential lessons from the chapters. In the second chapter, we discovered what the first two chapters of the book of Job say about sovereignty and suffering. The basic message being communicated is that God is Sovereign of all the suffering in your life.

This chapter is going to tackle Satan and suffering. This will not be a complete doctrine of Satan. That's not the point of the book of Job. I'm going to limit what I say to what these two chapters tell us about Satan. In doing so, I want to address two questions: what is the nature of Satan's attack and accusation on Job, and what lessons does this teach us?

SATAN'S STRATEGY WITH JOB

What was Satan's desire with Job? What was the nature of his attack and accusation on Job? Let's be reminded of the story by reading Job 1:6-12:

> Now there was a day when the sons of God came to present themselves before the LORD, and Satan also came among them. The LORD said to Satan, "From where do you come?" Then Satan answered the LORD and said, "From roaming about on the earth and walking around on it." The LORD said to Satan, "Have you considered My servant Job? For there is no one like him on the earth, a blameless and upright man, fearing God and turning away from evil." Then Satan answered the LORD, "Does Job fear God for nothing? Have You not made a fence around him and his house and all that he has, on every side? You have blessed the work of his hands, and his possessions have increased in the land. But put forth Your hand now and touch all that he has; he will certainly curse You to Your face." Then the LORD said to Satan, "Behold, all that he has is in your power; only do not put forth your hand on him." So Satan departed from the presence of the LORD.

We need to seriously consider the nature of Satan's intent. Satan is essentially saying that Job serves God because God has blessed him with health, wealth, and family. In other words, Satan accuses Job of treating God like a cosmic vending machine. If all Job had was taken away, his true heart would be revealed.

Though Satan is malicious in motives, his scheme does have merit. It's only when you lose something you love and trust that your true motivations and desires are exposed.

As Jon Bloom writes, "What we really love and trust aren't truly seen until we are tested by loss."[11] Of course, we know the story. Job proved to be faithful. Job showed that he was who he said he was—a worshipper of God, not self. But Satan is not done. He's never done. His plans continue until he gets what he wants. So Satan doubles down for round two, which we read about in Job 2:1-8:

> Again there was a day when the sons of God came to present themselves before the LORD, and Satan also came among them to present himself before the LORD. The LORD said to Satan, "Where have you come from?" Then Satan answered the LORD and said, "From roaming about on the earth and walking around on it." The LORD said to Satan, "Have you considered My servant Job? For there is no one like him on the earth, a blameless and upright man fearing God and turning away from evil. And he still holds firm to his integrity, although you incited Me against him to ruin him without cause." Satan answered the LORD and said, "Skin for skin! Yes, all that a man has, he will give for his life. However, put forth Your hand now, and touch his bone and his flesh; he will curse You to Your face!" So the LORD said to Satan, "Behold, he

---

11   Jon Bloom, *Don't Follow Your Heart: God's Ways Are Not Your Ways* (Minneapolis: Desiring God, 2015), 59.

> is in your power, only spare his life." Then Satan
> went out from the presence of the LORD and struck
> Job with severe boils from the sole of his foot to the
> crown of his head. And he took a potsherd to scrape
> himself while he was sitting among the ashes.

We see a lot of the same language here as we saw in the first chapter. What is different is Satan's accusation of "skin for skin." What does this mean? There are several ways people have understood what Satan is saying here. But at the end of the day, they all boil down to this: Satan desires to make a personal and bodily attack on Job.[12] In essence, Satan responds by saying that "God has not really touched Job where it hurts."[13] Satan, in other words, says, "Job is utterly selfish. You've taken away everything around him—family and finances, but You haven't taken away what he really cares about—his own life." Satan responds this way because killing Job would defeat his wicked purpose; it would take things too far. Job wouldn't be able to respond. Satan wanted Job harmed, not dead.

Here's the nature of Satan's attack: Satan's plan was to accuse Job. He aimed right at the heart motive. Satan made the accusation that Job's religion was fake, cheap, spoiled, and shallow. In short, his accusation was that Job served God for Job rather than serving God for God.

12   Anthony T. Selvaggio, *Considering Job: Reconciling Sovereignty & Suffering* (Grand Rapids: RHB, 2021), 41.
13   Richard P. Belcher Jr., *Job: The Mystery of Suffering and God's Sovereignty: Focus on the Bible* (Scotland: Christian Focus, 2017), 25.

SATAN'S STRATEGY TODAY

What does this teach us? Satan, as we have seen, is an accuser. In Revelation 12:10, the Bible calls him "the accuser of the brethren." In fact, the name "Satan" means accuser, opponent, or adversary. So what is he up to today? What wisdom lessons can we take away from the book of Job about Satan and suffering? At least four lessons can be learned.

LESSON 1: SATAN'S ACCUSATIONS SHOULD LEAD US TO EXAMINE OUR HEARTS[14]

God might ultimately allow Satan to harm you with suffering to test you to show what is in your heart. As Paul Tripp says, "Suffering doesn't so much change your heart as expose what has been in your heart all along."[15] Tripp gives this great example that helps make this concrete.

> Sarah had been plotted against and abandoned by her husband, she had lost custody of her children, and she had been left financially destitute. What had been done to her was horribly wrong, but her emotional and spiritual devastation was the result not only of the terrible wrongs that had been done to her but also of critical beliefs that she had carried into those wrongs. Sarah was a believer, but at street level, God was neither the source of her security nor her hope . . . It was the good life, not the gospel, that got her

---

14   Selvaggio, 29.
15   Paul David Tripp, *Suffering: Gospel Hope When Life Doesn't Make Sense* (Wheaton: Crossway, 2018), 34.

up every morning . . . The gospel of Jesus Christ was
her theology but didn't provide security for her heart
or drive the way that she lived. She understood that
she had been forgiven by grace and would spend an
eternity with the Lord, but there was a huge gap in
the middle of her grasp of the gospel. So, her life
became her personal messiah, giving her what it
was never meant to give. When Henry walked out
never to return and took literally everything with
him, Sarah didn't lose just Henry, the house, and the
kids—she lost herself. It was when Sarah got hold of
this truth that her heart began to lift, her hope began
to return, and she decided to live again.[16]

God wants Christians to experience true and lasting joy.
Sometimes, however, the blessings of life—even life itself—will
turn your heart away from God. We put God on the shelf. At best,
God becomes second place. But He cares too much about you to
let that happen. God is jealous of His own glory, and He is jealous
for you. God knows that the most satisfying and joy-filled life is
to know and enjoy God. So here is the reality—sometimes, God
takes so He can give. When you have everything but God, you have
nothing; when you have nothing but God, you have everything.

Suffering exposes your heart. Satan's accusations that come
with it should lead you to examine your heart. What brings you
the greatest joy, happiness, satisfaction, and comfort? Is it God or
is it something else? Unfortunately, you might not know until the

16 Tripp, 38-39.

suffering takes it away. The reality is, Satan's question can be asked of us: why do you serve God? Why do you do the things you do?

John Piper put this well when he asks a penetrating question. Here's my paraphrase of the question: if you could go to Heaven and have all the pleasures, joys, and happiness you could imagine—all the food, drink, sex, recreation, and toys—but Jesus wasn't there, would you still want to go?[17] Think about that question deeply. It reveals why you want God. It reveals why you claim to be a Christian.

Why are you a Christian? Why do you follow Jesus? Is it because of what He does for you? Is it because of the way it makes you feel or accepted in life? What if He took everything away? Perhaps God is allowing things to be taken away, and your heart is being exposed for what you are living for. This is exactly what we see Satan telling God, "Take it all away, and Job will turn from you. He will turn out to be a fraud!" If you recognize you are serving God for what He gives you, how do you turn from that attitude to loving God for God?

Suffering *exposes* your heart. But at the same time, suffering *refines* your heart. God becomes more beautiful and glorious to you because you love Him for Himself. It is no longer just about what He gives you. Although suffering's refining fire takes away material gifts, it is actually the process of God giving you Himself.

---

17   John Piper, *God is the Gospel: Meditations of God's Love as the Gift of Himself* (Wheaton: Crossway, 2005), 15.

This is what happened to a woman named Vaneetha. Vaneetha suffered four debilitating miscarriages. In her suffering and pain, God taught her He is her supreme Treasure. She writes this so well:

> When we worship and trust God in [a] trial, we declare that God is more valuable than anything he gives us. God, not our earthly blessings, is the ultimate object of our delight. Job continued to trust God after everything he had was destroyed, declaring, "The LORD gave and the LORD has taken away; blessed be the name of the LORD" (Job 1:21). While this response speaks highly of Job, it speaks far more highly of God. God is as worthy of our praise in times of loss, pain, and scarcity as He is in times of fruitfulness and abundance . . . [Through my suffering] I saw how linear my functional theology was—if I worshiped God and obeyed Him, I expected Him to give me what I wanted. And if I remained faithful through one big trial, He wouldn't keep letting me suffer. In my mind, the reward for following Jesus was a prosperous, fruit-filled, blessing-laden, trouble-free life. But as I saw in Job, God Himself is the reward. When we turn away from God in suffering, questioning His love and care, we are agreeing with Satan—that God's value is tied to the material blessings He gives us. And that is an immeasurable assault on God's worth.[18]

---

18   Vaneetha Rendall Risner, "The Lord Gave and Took Away: Lessons on Suffering from Job," Desiring God blog, October 9, 2021, https://www. desiringgod.org/articles/the-lord-gave-and-took-away.

If you are having a hard time in your life right now, perhaps God is exposing and refining your heart so that you worship God for Himself.

LESSON 2: SATAN'S ACCUSATIONS ARE ULTIMATELY ACCUSATIONS OF GOD[19]

Satan is accusing God of lying. God had said that Job is "a blameless and upright man, fearing God and turning away from evil" (Job 1:8). "Job is a good man," God says. Satan replies, "You lie, and I'll prove it to You. Make him suffer, and then You'll see."

In essence, what's happening here is Satan is doubting that a human being can express genuine faith in God. He doesn't think a human can follow God for God. Satan is doubting that God is powerful enough to change a self-worshipper—which you and I are by nature—into a God-worshipper. And when the Lord changes a self-worshipper to a God-worshipper, He gets all the glory. In essence, Satan is attacking the glory of God. He's attacking the very nature, the very deity, of God. Satan wants to dethrone God. He wants to rule. Satan's accusation and attack on you is ultimately an attack on God.[20]

LESSON 3: SATAN'S PLANS GO ONLY AS FAR AS GOD ALLOWS

As we saw in the last chapter, God is ultimately in charge in the book of Job. Satan accuses and desires to destroy you, but God

---

19   Selvaggio, 23.
20   Christopher Ash, *Job: The Wisdom of the Cross: Preach the Word* (Wheaton: Crossway, 2014), 45-46.

only allows it to go so far. In Job 1:12, God says to Satan: "Behold, all that he has is in your power; only do not put forth your hand on him." There's a limit. And in Job 2:6, God says, "'Behold, he is in Your power, only spare his life.'" Satan is on a leash. It's a long leash, be he is restrained, nonetheless. God permits Satan, as Peter says, to "[prowl] around like a roaring lion, seeking someone to devour" (1 Peter 5:8). But he only goes as far as God allows. When God says stop, Satan goes no further.

LESSON 4: SATAN'S ACCUSATIONS SHOULD LEAD YOU TO JESUS

God only allows Satan to go so far because Satan has ultimately been defeated. Jesus once told Peter: "Simon, Simon, behold, Satan has demanded *permission* to sift you like wheat" (Luke 22:31). Satan demanded to test and sift Peter and see what he was really made of. But Jesus goes on to say while He has permitted Satan to test Peter, He has "prayed for [him], that [his] faith will not fail" (Luke 22:32a).

Because of the Person and work of Jesus Christ, Satan can accuse and attack you; but the accusations ultimately cannot stick. When the fiery darts come flying in—the thoughts that you're a loser, that you'll never get your act together, that you're slated to commit the same sin over and over again, that you're doomed—you turn those thoughts to Jesus and say, "Therefore there is now no condemnation for those in Christ Jesus" (Rom. 8:1). Go to the cross. Go to Jesus. There the devil cannot stay!

CHAPTER 4

EMOTIONS AND SUFFERING

JOB 2:11-3:26

AS WE CONTINUE TO LOOK at the book of Job, we are building a theology of suffering. Each chapter of this book contributes a little bit more by way of "wisdom lessons" on suffering.

If you look at Job 3 in your copy of the Scripture, you will probably notice it is in block typesetting. That's because Job's words of lament are written in poetry. Poetry is the language of heart and emotions. Thus, poetry is meant to make you *feel* what you read. This style of writing is meant to engage your emotions. Interestingly, 95 percent of the book of Job is poetry. Job is not meant to be read in a stoic, heartless fashion. This portion of Scripture is written in such a way to make you feel the suffering and anguish of Job. Your emotions should be engaged. Job is a book you are meant to feel deep within. Job 13:25 and 13:28 are good examples of "feeling" poetry.

The reality is that when we suffer, there are two common emotions we feel—loneliness and lament. Job experienced both of these. The book of Job, therefore, beautifully offers more wisdom lessons, particularly on our emotions and suffering. Let's look at these lessons.

LESSON 1: SUFFERING PRODUCES FEELINGS OF LONELINESS

We can't miss or overlook the feelings of loneliness Job experienced during his suffering. Listen to a few of his own words from later in the book, as he is reflecting on his suffering. In Job 19:13-19, he says:

> "[God] has removed my brothers far from me, And my acquaintances are completely estranged from me. My relatives have failed, And my intimate friends have forgotten me. Those who live in my house and my maids consider me a stranger. I am a foreigner in their sight. I call to my servant, but he does not answer; I have to implore him with my mouth. My breath is offensive to my wife, And I am loathsome to my own brothers. Even young children despise me; I rise up and they speak against me. All my associates abhor me, And those I love have turned against me."

Job had brothers, relatives, employees, a wife, and children; but in his suffering, he feels alone. But that wasn't the worst of it. Job felt estranged from God Himself. It was not that Job felt that God had ruined his life but that he felt God had abandoned him. Listen to what Job says in Job 29:2-6:

"Oh that I were as in months gone by, As in the days when God watched over me; When His lamp shone over my head, *And* by His light I walked through darkness; As I was in the prime of my days, When the friendship of God *was* over my tent; When the Almighty was yet with me, *And* my children were around me; When my steps were bathed in butter, and the rock poured out for me streams of oil!"

Just as Job feels God's presence is gone, we, too, often feel alone in our suffering. Even if people are present with us, the darkness that suffering brings tends to make us feel alone. Loneliness manifests itself through statements like, "But you don't really understand what I'm going through."

LESSON 2: ONE OF THE BEST WAYS TO HELP SOMEONE SUFFERING IS TO GIVE THE MINISTRY OF PRESENCE

With Job, however, it was not *initially* loneliness he felt. The words from Job 19 and Job 29 occur after the friends open their mouths and begin to argue with him. Initially, when Job suffered, we see his friends come around to "sympathize and comfort him" in Job 2:11-13:

Now when Job's three friends heard of all this adversity that had come upon him, they came each one from his own place, Eliphaz the Temanite, Bildad the Shuhite and Zophar the Naamathite;

> and they made an appointment together to come
> to sympathize with him and comfort him. When
> they lifted up their eyes at a distance and did not
> recognize him, they raised their voices and wept.
> And each of them tore his robe and they threw dust
> over their heads toward the sky. Then they sat down
> on the ground with him for seven days and seven
> nights with no one speaking a word to him, for they
> saw that *his* pain was very great.

What Job's three friends initially offered him was the ministry of presence. Do you think about presence as a ministry? I marvel that Job's friends "sat down on the ground with him for seven days and seven nights with no one speaking a word to him" (Job 2:13a).

Loneliness is a major problem. And the irony is that with all the "connections" in our modern world, studies show there has never been a time where people have felt so lonely. The COVID-19 pandemic made loneliness worse, especially in the early days when we had to quarantine from one another. One of my friends described almost going crazy while self-isolating for ten days. Now we know a little bit why solitary confinement is a harsh form of punishment. Human beings were made to have relationships with one another.

Selvaggio has this to say about suffering: "Suffering is hard. Suffering alone is harder."[21] "Suffering," as one says, "is not a

---

21   Selvaggio, 46.

question that requires an answer; a problem that requires a solution; it's a mystery that requires a presence."[22]

Think about it like this. The Lord establishes His Presence among His people. In the early days of wandering in the wilderness, He establishes the tabernacle so that He can be present with His people. The principle of presence continued with the construction of the temple in Jerusalem, a place where He dwells with His people. And, of course, the principle of presence continues when the Son of God enters the world as Immanuel—God with us (Matt. 1:22-23). Jesus came and dwelt among His people (John 1:14). Now, we have the continuing indwelling presence of the Holy Spirit (1 Cor. 3:16, 6:19; 2 Cor. 6:16; 2 Tim. 1:14). The ministry of the presence of God is a major theme throughout the Bible.

Don't despise the ministry of presence. When you are with someone in their suffering, your presence sometimes means more than words could ever say. I recently went through a period of suffering and deep depression in my own life. The presence of my wife, parents, brother, friends, and pastors meant the world to me. Their presence alone helped me get better. When a friend or family member is suffering, don't feel like you have to say something. Don't feel like you have to fix them or their suffering. As Romans 12:15 beautifully and simply puts it, we are to "weep with those who weep."

---

22   Source of quote is unknown.

However, though presence is important, it does not automatically end a person's suffering. The presence of Job's friends, though helpful for seven days, had its limits. The end of Job 2 says "*his* pain was very great" (v. 13). After the seven days, Job expressed deep lament for his suffering.

In the previous chapters, we have looked at what happened to Job. Now, in chapter three, we see inside Job.[23] Let's read and reflect on his emotional lament:

> Afterward Job opened his mouth and cursed the day of his *birth*. And Job said, "Let the day perish on which I was to be born, And the night *which* said, 'A boy is conceived.' May that day be darkness; Let not God above care for it, Nor light shine on it. Let darkness and black gloom claim it; Let a cloud settle on it; Let the blackness of the day terrify it. *As for* that night, let darkness seize it; Let it not rejoice among the days of the year; Let it not come into the number of the months. Behold, let that night be barren; Let no joyful shout enter it. Let those curse it who curse the day, Who are prepared to rouse Leviathan. Let the stars of its twilight be darkened; Let it wait for light but have none, And let it not see the breaking dawn; Because it did not shut the opening of my *mother's* womb, Or hide trouble from my eyes" (Job 3:1-10).

---

23   Ash, 69.

Job goes on to question his birth and says that death is better than suffering. Wow! This man was suffering. I want to draw a third lesson we learn from this lament.

LESSON 3: EMOTION IS NOT IN ITSELF SINFUL

What I find particularly instructive for us is that Job's lament is not regarded as sinful. In fact, we know from the first two chapters of Job that "Job did not sin nor did he blame God" (Job 1:22), even though we see him tear his robe and shave his head, which were signs of intense grief and mourning (Job 1:20). Even the end of the book confirms that Job spoke of God what is right (Job 42:7-8).

Job 3:1 tells us that instead of cursing God, Job cursed the day of his birth. Job, like a genie granting three wishes, laments three realities in the broken world: wishing he had never been born or conceived (Job 3:3-10), wishing he had died in the womb (Job 3:11-19), and wishing that those who suffer might die quickly (Job 3:20-26).[24] With these three wishes expressed in this lament, Job certainly asks a lot of questions. But at this point, he is not angry at God. Neither is Job complaining here. The difference between lament and complaining is that "lamenting is a cry for God; complaining is a cry against God."[25] Job did not sin.

The emotions of suffering—lament, sorrow, sadness, grief, groaning, weeping, sobbing, and even depression—are

---

24   David R. Jackson, *Crying out for Vindication: The Gospel According to Job* (Phillipsburg: P&R, 2007), 55.

25   Tchividjian, 165.

not necessarily sinful, nor do they represent a lack of faith. Unfortunately, we can go to two extremes with emotions.

First, we may try to minimize our emotions and try hard to numb feelings of pain. We can do this through substances, food, entertainment, escape, and many other ways. We also try, with good intentions, to numb the pain of others when we tell sufferers things like, "Don't listen to your feelings. Don't be guided by your feelings. Do what you know is right, regardless of how you feel." There is truth to these statements. Your feelings don't override or cancel truth. But minimizing our emotions shortcuts us an opportunity to learn from these emotions and lean into God in the face of emotion. "Pour out your heart before Him" (Ps. 62:8). Squashing, ignoring, numbing, or suppressing emotions is not a biblical approach. Your emotions are important. They are designed and given as a gift by God.

The other extreme is to maximize your emotions and let them rule the day. We could call this emotionalism. When we maximize our emotions, fact and faith are interpreted through emotions and feelings guide our lives. The engine of our personal train is driven by how we *feel* not by fact and faith. Our twenty-first century postmodern world is driven by emotionalism. "Follow your heart" is a common mantra of our day. Even the Christian church can be ruled and guided by emotions rather than Scripture.

So, on the one hand, the solution is not to minimize your or another's emotions by playing the "God is Sovereign" trump card. Yes, as I said in an earlier chapter, God is Sovereign over all the suffering in your life. This truth does bring comfort in suffering. However, on the other hand, the "God is Sovereign" trump card must be used wisely and winsomely, not to squelch what a person is feeling. Too many Christians, trying to help, say that your problem is that you just need to trust God. While this *may* be true that you need to trust God, people should not use it as a "magic pill" to erase the emotions a person feels during suffering. At the same time, the solution *may* be that you need to trust God. Don't let your emotions run your life. Don't let your emotions dictate how you behave.

Can you sense the emotions Job had? I know I can certainly sympathize with him! Let me remind you of his physical suffering with descriptions from the book of Job itself: fever with chills (Job 21:6), darkening and shriveling of the skin (Job 30:30), red eyes swollen from weeping (Job 16:16), diarrhea (Job 30:27), sleeplessness and delirium (Job 7:4, 13-14), bad breath (Job 19:17), emaciation (Job 19:20), and excruciating pain throughout the body (Job 30:17).[26] I feel sorry for him—I really do. As Andersen says: Job's "skin is festering, and his nerves are on fire."[27]

Ever been there? Sure. We all have—maybe not to the extent of Job, but you may be there right now. It's okay to mourn, cry, and grieve. Happy, clappy Christianity is not real, and it is not

---

26   Belcher, Jr., 26.
27   Andersen, 108.

what God expects. "The Lord's testing," writes Anderson, "is not to find out if Job can sit unmoved like a piece of wood."[28]

Instead of minimizing or maximizing your emotions, *evaluate* them. Here are three questions you can ask yourself: What emotions am I feeling? Why am I feeling this way? What do my emotions tell me about the state of my heart?

Your emotions reveal where your heart is. They tell you what is happening inside. As Paul Tripp writes in his excellent book on suffering, "Your suffering is more powerfully shaped by what's in your heart than by what's in your body or in the world around you."[29] Use your emotions to evaluate where your heart is. Allow your emotions to draw you to God in lament and in praise. Lament and grief are not opposites of praise and worship. They are also not signs of unbelief and doubt. These emotions are actually what God designed in appropriate situations. As the wisdom of Ecclesiastes teaches us, there is "[a] time to weep and a time to laugh; a time to mourn and a time to dance" (Eccl. 3:4). Job did both lament and worship at the same time. Job worshipped *in* his grief, not *because* of his grief.

Job is in a seemingly hopeless situation. That's where suffering may have you, but you don't need to stay there. Because of the gospel, there is hope in your suffering, which brings us to our final lesson.

---

28   Ibid.
29   Tripp, 31.

LESSON 4: JESUS EXPERIENCED LONELINESS AND LAMENT TO DELIVER YOU FROM THESE EMOTIONS

As Christians, we need to read the book of Job through a "Jesus lens." We must see Jesus in Job. Christ Himself experienced loneliness and lament. At the tomb of His friend Lazarus, Jesus didn't say, "Don't weep, Mary, look what I'm about to do." No, "Jesus wept" (John 11:35). In the garden of Gethsemane, while with His three friends, Jesus begged them to stay and pray. They fell asleep, and Jesus prayed and wept alone (Matt. 26:36-46). Just a little while later, during His most intense suffering on the cross, He cried out: "'MY GOD, MY GOD, WHY HAVE YOU FORSAKEN ME'" (Matt. 27:46)? Now, we must understand Jesus' abandonment on the cross does not mean that the Trinity ceased to exist, that the Father ceased to love the Son, or that Jesus lost faith in the Father. It meant Jesus was bearing the sins of His people. In that horrific moment, the Father could not look on the Son due to the sin He was bearing.

What I want you to see is that Jesus suffered the brunt of the Father's wrath for sinners like you and me. In fact, He experienced an infinite loneliness that Job—or you and I—will never experience as Christians. He cried out in lament, so your mourning will be turned into joy. He was forsaken, feeling intense loneliness, so He will never leave us or forsake us (Heb. 13:5). This is the power of the cross. This is the power of the gospel.

You see, Jesus not only sympathizes with us (Heb. 4:15), but He also knows the range of emotions we experience. He experienced loneliness and lament so that one day both painful emotions would ultimately be removed from us. It is no wonder that Revelation tells us one day every tear will be wiped from our eyes (Rev. 7:17). In Heaven, we will never experience loneliness or lament again. This is the hope that Job's loneliness and lament points to. This is our hope as believers and followers of Jesus.

CHAPTER 5

SIN AND SUFFERING

JOB 4:1-27:23

IT'S BEEN THREE MONTHS SINCE the pain started. The wait is finally over. You make it to your appointment on time . . . and wait. Finally, with your heart racing and your palms sweating, a nurse calls your name and escorts you to the room. It is freezing cold, and the lights are brighter than the noonday sun. You're handed a piece of cloth, and she tells you to take everything off and put on an ugly-looking robe. She exits the room. You sigh.

For the next five minutes, you struggle to tie the piece of cloth around your backside; but eventually, you get it on. You sit on the table, anxiously waiting for the knock. The knock comes. The doctor enters. He examines you and then says words that you've dreaded for months: "I think we need to do some more tests. What I'm seeing does not look good."[30]

---

30 This example was adapted from Selvaggio, 1.

Where does your heart go in this moment? What runs through your thoughts? This scenario, though scary, pales in comparison to what Job went through.

WHY DOES GOD ALLOW SUFFERING?

Job suffered greatly, and I feel bad for Job—I really do. He made the right decisions. He took care of his family physically and spiritually. He lived within his means. He was careful and godly. Yet this man suffered financially, physically, emotionally, mentally, and relationally. Every aspect of his life he lost—except his life. It's much worse to lose everything except your life. When you lose your life, as a Christian, you gain glory. When you lose everything except your life, it seems like you gain nothing but suffering.

There is a nagging question I have if I really care about what happened to Job, and I am really concerned about the suffering I see in this life. Why the suffering? What did they, or I, do to deserve this?

When suffering strikes, we always look for answers and justice. We want to know why suffering happens, and we especially desire to know if it is deserved. You could say, "It is not suffering that destroys a man, but suffering without a purpose."[31] After seven days of silence, Job's friends open their mouths and offer a reason why Job is suffering. Obviously, they have good intentions, but they totally miss the target.

---

31   Christopher Ash, *Trusting God in the Darkness: A Guide to Understanding the Book of Job* (Wheaton: Crossway, 2021), 46.

SUFFERING MUST BE THE RESULT OF PERSONAL SIN

Over half of the book of Job is the discussion between Job and his three friends. The arguments run from Job 4 through Job 27, with some summary statements by Job in Job 28-31. Then another friend enters the scene in Job 32.

The content covered in Job 4-27 is somewhat repetitive. In fact, we can boil all these speeches down to one basic argument. Here is the essential argument which Job's three friends—Eliphaz, Bildad, and Zophar—make over and over again: Since God is fair and just, He must punish sin; therefore, since you are suffering, God must be punishing you for your sin.

We see their argument right from the beginning. In fact, if you look at chapter four in a Bible, some of you might see a heading: "Eliphaz: The Innocent Do Not Suffer." This heading aptly summarizes Eliphaz's argument: "Remember now, who *ever* perished being innocent? Or were the upright destroyed?" (Job 4:7). The implied answer is no one. He is saying to Job, "If you were innocent, Job, you would not be suffering."

Now notice chapter five: "But as for me, I would seek God, And I would place my cause before God; Who does great and unsearchable things, Wonders without number" (Job 5:8-9). In other words, why would anyone place their case before God? He is just, and He will surely do what is right. According to Job's friends, this is the cause for his suffering. He is being punished for his sins.

Eliphaz even goes on to say that Job's suffering is the *discipline* of the Lord. "Behold, now happy is the man whom God reproves, so do not despise the discipline of the Almighty'" (Job 5:17). Do these words ring a bell for you? If you know your Bible, Eliphaz's words echo a verse found in the New Testament. Hebrews 12:5 says, "[And] you have forgotten the exhortation which is addressed to you as sons, 'MY SON, DO NOT REGARD LIGHTLY THE DISCIPLINE OF THE LORD, NOR FAINT WHEN YOU ARE REPROVED BY HIM.'"

In summary, Job's friends conclude that Job has sinned. Is their argument valid and true? The logic is correct. But is it true? Let's answer the question biblically.

SUFFERING IS NOT NECESSARILY THE RESULT OF PERSONAL SIN

The Bible is clear in the book of Genesis that because of Adam and Eve's sin, suffering entered the world. All suffering is a result of sin; suffering is a result of the Fall. To clarify, all suffering is the result of sin, but not all suffering is the result of individual sin. This is not a contradiction because I am equivocating in my language. What do I mean? All suffering is the result of sin in general, but not all suffering is the result of sin in particular. What I mean by this is that you can't draw a straight line from someone's personal sin—the sin that they have done—to the suffering that they are going through.

Jesus forcefully and powerfully illustrates this point in the book of John. "As He passed by, He saw a man blind from birth. And His disciples asked Him, 'Rabbi, who sinned, this man or his parents that he would be born blind?' Jesus answered, '*It was* neither *that* this man sinned, nor his parents; but *it was* so that the works of God might be displayed in him'" (John 9:1-3). What is the point? It's not because of *personal* sin of the son or his parents for why the lad suffered with blindness.

Now, this is one example, and I'm hesitant to draw a universal principle or rule from one example. But at least John 9 is *one* place where we have an example that suffering is not the result of personal sin. This isn't the only place. We can also see this in the book of Job.

The narrator makes it clear that Job's suffering is not a result of his personal sin. Look at Job 1:1: "There was a man in the land of Uz whose name was Job; and that man was *blameless, upright, fearing God and turning away from evil*" (emphasis added). Even *after* Job suffered, he did not sin. Job 1:22 tells us, "Through all this [suffering] Job did not sin nor did he blame God." And in Job 2:10, we read, "But [Job] said to [his wife], 'You speak as one of the foolish women speaks. Shall we indeed accept good from God and not accept adversity?' In all this Job did not sin with his lips." The narrator is clear about Job. He is *not* suffering because of his personal sin.

Let me give you a modern-day example that may help you understand. A few years ago, I learned from a pastor friend about some horrible suffering that a family in his church was going through. A son took his father's gun in hand, but he didn't know that it was loaded. In jest, he pointed the gun at his sister, pulled the trigger, and killed his sister. The suffering is unreal. I cannot even scratch the surface of suffering in this situation. Here's my question: who sinned to bring on all this suffering? Is my friend going to start pointing fingers?

So, are Job's friends correct? Again, their argument is that God is just and fair in all that He does. Because of this, He cannot overlook sin. All sin must be punished; and because Job was suffering, it must mean that Job had sinned. Is this true?

Here's my answer. What the friends say is true, but it's not true for Job. They assume he is suffering for personal sin. As Eric Ortlund says, the friends "turn a general principle of cause and effect into an ironclad rule in which the effect always and only shows the cause. But herein lies their mistake, for while it is true that we reap what we sow, it is not true that we reap only what we sow. Sin always causes suffering, but not all suffering is caused by particular sin."[32] In reality, the problem with Job's friends is that they have no place in their theology for innocent suffering. Even worse, Job's friends have no understanding of grace.

THE CROSS, SIN, AND SUFFERING

In 1989, Auschwitz survivor Harold Kushner wrote a best-selling book, *When Bad Things Happen to Good People.* The book was his attempt to wrestle with sin and suffering in the world.

---

32   Eric Ortlund, *Piercing Leviathan: God's Defeat of Evil in the Book of Job–New Studies in Biblical Theology* (Downers Grove: InterVarsity Press, 2021), 76. Kindle.

People often ask, "Why do bad things like suffering happen to good people?" As Christians, we believe the premise is flawed. "Bad things happen," we say, "because no one is good. The real question should be why good things happen to bad people." But I'm not convinced the premise is flawed. Is there such a thing as good people? Is there such a thing as innocent suffering?

Let me ask it like this: was Job a sinner? Yes, of course he was. If he wasn't, then the rest of the Bible would not be true. Scripture must interpret Scripture. What I'm saying is that the book of Job presents a man who suffers and whose suffering is not tied to a specific sin he has done. In other words, Job, in a certain way, is an innocent sufferer. Job was not suffering because of his *personal* sins.

This concept of an innocent sufferer should shout and scream to you about the life of another innocent sufferer. Jesus entered our broken world. He suffered throughout His life and, even greater, at His death. Was Jesus a sinner? No, He was innocent. He was truly innocent—personally—and He did not have a sin nature. Bad things happened to a perfectly good Person.

Yet the irony is that Jesus suffered not because He was a sinner; He suffered because He was a Savior. Jesus' suffering in life and on the cross is because of sin in the world. He didn't deserve the suffering; He didn't deserve the punishment. But on the cross, Jesus took your sin, if you are a Christian. He took the sin that you deserve to suffer for. Jesus came to end sin and suffering.

GRACE, SIN, AND SUFFERING[33]

Also, because Job's friends have no cross, they do not understand grace. "In a Peanuts' cartoon Lucy says to Charlie Brown, 'There is one thing you're going to have to learn: you reap what you sow; you get out of life what you put into it, no more or no less.' Snoopy musters from the corner, 'I'd kind of like to see a little margin for error.'"[34]

Job's friends take the position of Lucy. Look at Job 4:8: "According to what I have seen, those who plow iniquity And those who sow trouble harvest it." Job, in other words, deserves suffering because he has plowed iniquity, so he reaps suffering. Listen to Eliphaz's words in Job 5:6: "For affliction does not come from the dust, Nor does trouble sprout from the ground." You know what he is saying? "Suffering doesn't happen naturally. It happens because you, Job, earned it. You deserve it."

Now, is it true that you reap what you sow (Gal. 6:7)? Is it true that God has built into the fabric of the world a basic principle that if you work hard and do the right thing, you will be rewarded? Yes, this is true in a general sense. But according to Snoopy, it leaves no room for a margin of error.

We live with a merit-based mentality. If you want to succeed in life, you need to pump up your résumé. You need to have qualifications, training, and experience. To get into a good college, you need to perform with good grades and ACT test

---

33   Keller, 276.
34   Ash, 95.

scores. Scholarships are awarded for merit. This is how life works in the West. This is our culture and what we expect. I know this is our culture because what happens when we don't make the grade, don't have the résumé, or fail the test?

Job's friends do not understand grace. Their day is ordered by a regimen of do's and don'ts. They judge by a system of performance. They live by a rigid code of law. But the reality is that God is not obligated to bless you or reward your good work and uprightness. This would not be grace. Grace, in order for it to be grace, is under no obligation. We *have* blown it. We *have* sinned against God. Job did, too. It's not why he was suffering, but he was a sinner. Job was not suffering because he had blown it; he was suffering because God wanted to prove Job's character. Job was suffering because even when life doesn't work the way it's supposed to and what you sow is not what you reap, God gives grace.

I'm thankful for a "margin of error" because, without it, you and I would be blown to pieces by God's just and righteous wrath. It is true what Job's friends say about God. He is just. All sin must be punished. But grace means you get what you don't deserve. You get an innocent sufferer who made atonement in your place. So we rejoice.

CHAPTER 6
COUNSEL AND SUFFERING

JOB 4:1–27:23

IN THE EARLY EIGHTEENTH CENTURY, the American Puritan Pastor Cotton Mather was instrumental in the initial stages of what would later become a vaccine against smallpox disease. Of course, there have always been naysayers for vaccinations. In fact, Mather's opponents said that smallpox was God's Divine judgment on people, and they quoted Job 2:7 in support: "Then Satan went out from the presence of the LORD and smote Job with sore boils from the sole of his foot to the crown of his head."[35]

I am not making any sort of comment on vaccines. My point is Mather's opponents attributed the disease of smallpox to Divine judgment and punishment for sins. This is exactly what Job's friends did.

---

35 Seth Mnookin, *The Panic Virus: The True Story Behind the Vaccine-Autism Controversy* (New York: Simon and Schuster, 2011), 25.

THE COUNSEL OF JOB'S THREE FRIENDS

Now, whether Job suffered from smallpox is unknown. What we do know is that the man suffered a great deal. And his interlocutors attributed his suffering to Divine judgment for his sins. Essentially, the proposed solution as to why Job was suffering was because he had sinned. Their basic argument went like this: God is just and fair in all that He does. Because God is just and fair in all that He does, He must punish sin. Therefore, "Job, you are suffering (being punished and disciplined) because you have sinned in some way." There is truth to what his friends are suggesting. God is just and righteous and will punish sins. The problem with the friends, however, is that their answer was not true for Job.

And because their basic reason for Job's suffering was Job had sinned, their basic counsel to him is this, "Repent! Confess your sins to the Lord." In Job 8:5-6, they admonish him, "If you would seek God and implore the compassion of the Almighty; If you are pure and upright, Surely now He would rouse Himself for you And restore your righteous estate." These friends are telling Job that he needs to turn back to God and live righteously.

Job, however, is not convinced. He will have nothing to do with their solutions or counsel. For him, the words of his friends are unhelpful and worthless. "Then Job answered, 'I have heard many such things; Sorry comforters are you all'" (Job 16:1-2). Job feels like he can't win. If he tries to defend himself of wrongdoing or sinning, he gets hammered by his friends. If he doesn't defend himself, he just suffers, especially under the weight of his friend's counsel. "If I speak, my pain is not lessened, And if I hold back, what has left me" (Job 16:6)? But Job knows that he is not suffering because he sinned. Job 9:21-22 says, "I am guiltless; I do not take notice of myself; I despise my life. It is *all* one; therefore I say, *'He destroys the guiltless and the wicked'*" (emphasis added). It's not the blameless who do not suffer. There is such a thing as innocent suffering.

HOW THE COUNSEL OF JOB'S FRIENDS WENT WRONG

The counsel of Job's friends missed the mark. Fundamentally, the problem with Job's friends is that they had no category for an innocent sufferer. Yes, they knew Job was a saint and a sinner. But it is precisely *because of* his sin that they believe he is suffering. Job's friends had no category for innocent suffering— that is, suffering that is not tied to specific sin that has been done. And because they had no category for innocent sufferer in their theology, this led them to give the wrong counsel to Job in their practice. If the diagnosis is wrong, the treatment is wrong. Here is where their counsel went wrong.

First, they show no compassion or sympathy toward Job.[36] They are more interested in a lecture than loving a man broken from suffering. They are more interested in being right than ministering to a man in his pain. Look what Eliphaz says in

---

36   Ash, 93-98.

Job 4:2-5: "If one ventures a word with you, will you become impatient? But who can refrain from speaking? Behold you have admonished many, and you have strengthened weak hands. Your words have helped the tottering to stand, And you have strengthened feeble knees. But now it has come to you, and you are impatient; It touches you, and you are dismayed."

In other words, "Job, you have helped others in suffering but now it has come to you, and you can't help yourself. Why can't you fix yourself, Job?" Not really the first thing you should say to someone suffering!

This reminds me of a story I read. A woman once came to her pastor with severe chronic health problems. After listening for a few moments, he stopped her in her tracks and began to offer what he considered to be correct theological statements. And they were. But after his diatribe, she said to him: "I didn't come to you because I expected you to have answers. I simply wanted you to listen to me."[37] Ouch! Ministering to sufferers requires compassion and care, not winning debates or proving you're right.

The second point is related to the first. Job's friends feel superior to him. In Job 11:12, Zophar suggests Job is an idiot. Eliphaz basically says, "If I were you, I'd . . . " Here are his words, "But as for me, I would seek God, And I would place my cause before God" (Job 5:8). The problem with this advice is that people who are suffering are seldom able to hear such an attitude of

---

37   Selvaggio, 96-97.

superiority, no matter how right it is. Job's friends were right in some ways; but in others, they were so wrong. Job's friends ultimately lack the humility needed to care for him. It reminds me of what I read about James Dobson. Dobson once said, "I used to have four theories on child-rearing and no kids. Now I have four kids and no theories."[38] This is a statement of humility.

Job lost his family, his wealth, and his health. He had enough suffering with these losses. But the friends, as it sometimes goes, added to his suffering. This is not how we should respond to a sufferer. Job's friends are a lesson in what not to do. How then can you help someone who is suffering?

A FRAMEWORK FOR COUNSEL: SAINT, SINNER, AND SUFFERER

The Bible presents the Christian in a three-fold state—that of saint, sinner, and sufferer. The Bible is full of this framework, but one example is in Romans 6-8. Here we find all three of these categories are on display. Romans pictures the Christian as a saint. Listen to Romans 6:6-7, where Paul says to Christians, "knowing this, that our old self was crucified with *Him*, in order that our body of sin might be done away with, so that we would no longer be slaves to sin; for he who has died is freed from sin." You are a saint.

But saints still sin, as Paul attests in Romans 7:18-19: "For I know that nothing good dwells in me, that is, in my flesh; for the

---

38   Ash, 94.

willing is present in me, but the doing of the good *is* not. For the good that I want, I do not do, but I practice the very evil that I do not want." Even though we are saints, we still struggle with sin.

Finally, in Romans 8:18 and 22, Paul says "that the sufferings of this present time are not worthy to be compared with the glory that is to be revealed to us . . . For we know that the whole creation groans and suffers the pains of childbirth together until now." In Romans 6, we are saints; in Romans 7, we are sinners; and in Romans 8, we are sufferers. That's just one example in Scripture.

So, to offer any counsel or advice to Christians, we *must* recognize this biblical framework of the Christian life. We must have a category for innocent suffering in our counsel. Not everything fits into the category of saint or sinner. Sometimes you suffer; and it's not because you have done wrong, God is trying to teach you a lesson, or God is letting your past come back to haunt you. You live in a broken world with suffering everywhere.

Christians and churches can get the gospel right. They can "dot all the i's and cross all the t's." But a Christian or a church that cares about doctrine can sometimes easily miss the category of sufferer. As a result, we can be like Job's friends and have no sympathy and compassion for those suffering, even when they are suffering because of someone's sins! We can tend to offer theological diatribes and statements but not care about the person. Suffering is chalked up to sin. If you are suffering in a marriage to an unbeliever, it's because of your sin. Your cancer is because of your sin. The difficult relationship is because of your sin. You lost your job because of your sin.

You might be thinking to yourself, "I'm not a counselor. In fact, I am deathly afraid of counseling." Let me just say that if you have a pulse, you are a counselor! Every one of us has relationships: spouse, children, colleagues, neighbors, and church members. We all have influence on someone. As Christians, we are disciple-making disciples. As Paul Tripp says, we are "people in need of change helping people in need of change."[39]

SIMULTANEOUSLY A SAINT, A SINNER, AND A SUFFERER

But one more point needs to be made clear. Christians are saints, sinners, and sufferers all at the *same time*. Every Christian is simultaneously a saint, sinner, and sufferer. Because this is the case, it is extremely difficult in the minutia and messiness of life to tease out which parts of a person's life fall into which category. Let me give you an example.

John had been a Christian for about fifteen years. He became a saint the moment he became a believer. Sainthood is not something that is achieved in life through miracles and good works. Recently, however, John's wife betrayed him and left him for another man. John is devastated. John turns to drinking to escape the pain: every day after work, He heads to

---

39   Tripp, *Instruments in the Redeemer's Hands*.

the bar to drink his troubles away. John became aloof, alone, and spiraled into deep depression, which leads him to seek counseling from his pastor.

John is a saint, sinner, and sufferer *at the same time.* In your counsel, you cannot neglect one category for the other two categories. When you ignore one for the other, here is what can happen. (I have been helped here by Christian counselor, Mike Emlet.)[40]

When you overemphasize the experience as saint, you can tend to minimize or downplay wrongdoing, responsibility, and progressive growth in godliness. In John's case, this might be giving him a pass on his drinking problem because, after all, look at what has happened to him. Give the guy a break!

When you overemphasize the experience as sinner, you can tend to focus on what needs to change at the expense of seeing all that God has done or focusing on law-keeping, rules, and commands rather than the heart and a personal relationship with Christ. In John's case, this might entail lecturing him on why drunkenness is a sin and making a list of rules that he must follow to avoid drinking.

When you overemphasize the experience as sufferer, you can tend to have a victim mentality, trying to escape suffering through ungodly and unbiblical means. In John's case, this might entail empowering him to feel angry at his wife's behavior where no

---

40   Michael R. Emlet, *Saints, Sufferers, and Sinners: Loving Others as God Loves Us* (Greensboro: New Growth Press, 2020), 130-35. Kindle.

personal responsibility is taken in the marriage and no forgiveness is given. Though this is a fictitious, simple example for illustration purposes, matters in real life are incredibly complex. What is the true source of John's problems as a saint, sinner, and sufferer? This is why in any counsel to John, we must remember he is always a saint, sinner, and sufferer *at the same time*. We must not neglect one category for the other two. So how do you help someone like John in their suffering?

PRACTICAL GUIDANCE TO HELP THE SUFFERER

I am going to lean on the wisdom and experience of Mike Emlet again. Here are some questions and strategies that you can implement:

Questions to ask of the person as a sufferer, which is all Christians to one degree or another:

- What significant situational stressors are they currently facing? These would include but are not limited to physical issues or relational, cultural, or social influences.
- What significant events have shaped their life?
- How have they been sinned against?
- How are they experiencing their problems?[41]

---

41   Michael R. Emlet, *Cross Talk: Where Life & Scripture Meet* (Greensboro: New Growth Press, 2009), 96-97. Kindle.

Now, some things to consider:

- Take the suffering of others seriously.
- Work hard to understand the details of their suffering.
- Don't presume you know the reason(s) for their suffering.
- Give them a lot of biblical encouragement and hope.[42]
- Be present and listen well.
- Pray with them and for them.

Based on these questions, it could be with our example of John that suffering *might* be predominant in his life right now. As far as we can tell, the betrayal of John's wife is not the result of any specific sin or action on John's part. This does not mean that John did not contribute his own sin to the marriage. The man, however, is suffering a great loss. Therefore, it *might* be, and often is helpful, to address John's suffering before you address John's sin. With any counsel, we must remember that these categories—saint, sinner, sufferer—and address them one by one.

JESUS AS A SAINT, A "SINNER," AND A SUFFERER[43]

All our counseling, however, is not done in a vacuum. It is done in light of Jesus and the cross. This chapter wouldn't be

---

42   Emlet, 63-66, 69.
43   Emlet, 16-19.

complete without pointing out the fact that our Lord Jesus is Himself the ultimate saint, "sinner," and sufferer. If we read it rightly, the book of Job points to this truth.

Jesus is the ultimate Saint. He is declared many times in Scripture to be the beloved Son of God (Matt. 3:17, 16:16, 17:5; Rom. 1:4). Not only is this Christ's identity as a Person, but His life was marked by sainthood. He kept the law of God perfectly. He obeyed His Father, even at great cost to Himself. If there ever was a saint, it was—and is—Jesus.

Jesus is also the ultimate "Sinner." I use this term in quotes, so I'm not accused of false teaching. Jesus did not experience sin in the same way we do. Hebrews 4:15 says He was tempted in every way like we are, but He never sinned. Jesus, however, became sin for us on the cross. Paul is clear about this in 2 Corinthians 5:21: "He made Him who knew no sin *to be* sin on our behalf, so that we might become the righteousness of God in Him." In this way, all the sins of God's people were placed on Christ. The theological word for this is imputation. He became the cursed—the sin curse—on the tree (Gal. 3:13). Jesus never personally sinned; but in the wisdom of God, He became sin. He felt the full weight of the wrath of God against sin in His body on the cross. In this way, He was the ultimate "Sinner" because He was the sin-bearer for every single Christian of all time.

Jesus is the ultimate Sufferer. He entered a broken world. He suffered, just like we all do, from day one of His earthly existence as both God and man. This is why Isaiah pictures Jesus as the suffering Servant (Isa. 52-53). Paul says Jesus "emptied Himself, taking the form a bond-servant, *and* being made in the likeness of men" (Phil. 2:7). The writer of Hebrews says that Jesus learned obedience through what He suffered (Heb. 5:8). He is the ultimate Sufferer because He had everything and became nothing for us.

What does all this mean? It means that in your suffering, you can turn to the One Who knew suffering and suffered in your place. This is why I love when the author of Hebrews says that Jesus is not an *unsympathetic* High Priest. In the face of friends who show no sympathy, know that Jesus will. Sympathy is His heart for the saint, sinner, and sufferer.

This also means that because Jesus suffered, you—as a Christian—can offer counsel to friends and loved ones in the face of their suffering. This is the wisdom that the book of Job ultimately affords us. In view of Jesus, learn to see others as saints, sinners, and sufferers and give caring, loving counsel in this light.

CHAPTER 7

WISDOM AND SUFFERING

JOB 28:1-28

THERE IS A CLASSIC, VIRTUALLY wordless Calvin and Hobbes comic strip that sums up what life often feels like. The comic is a series of panels, each depicting a scene all from one day. First, Calvin sits on a wad of bubble gum. Next, his teacher catches him glancing at his classmate's test. Then a bully knocks him down in the hallway. The water fountain sprays in his face. The bug he'd brought in for show-and-tell escapes. He gets picked last at recess. There's a hair in his lunch; and when he heads to the swing set, all the seats are occupied. Finally, he misses the bus and must walk home in the rain. In his bedroom that evening, Calvin looks at his trusted tiger and says, "You know, Hobbes, some days even my lucky rocket ship underpants don't help."[44]

I think we need more than lucky rocket ship underpants. Although they do help! Life is hard because life is full of

---

44   Tchividjian, 59.

suffering. What we need in the face of suffering—both personal suffering and the suffering of others—is deep-seated wisdom. And in a way, that is why the book of Job has been written. It's a story—a true story—that conveys more than facts about a man named Job and his suffering. This story conveys wisdom for life in a broken world.

So far in the last six chapters, we have learned different lessons in wisdom from the book of Job—lessons about the believer and suffering, sovereignty and suffering, Satan and suffering, emotions and suffering, sin and suffering, and counsel and suffering. As helpful as these wisdom lessons have been, there is a sense in which they have been incomplete without one of Job's final comments in chapter twenty-eight.

This chapter is almost like an aside in the flow of the book of Job. But it is an important aside because it teaches us something very important about wisdom in suffering. And I'm so thankful for Job 28 because wisdom sometimes seems elusive; it appears hard to grasp. We desperately need wisdom, but where do we find it? How does it come about?

WHERE IS WISDOM FOUND?

This is exactly the question Job asks! Where is wisdom found? "But where can wisdom be found? And where is the place of understanding" (Job 28:12)? He desperately wants to know, so he asks it again in verse twenty, "Where then does wisdom come from? And where is the place of understanding?" The questions lead us to an answer. But before we can get to an answer, as a good rhetorical device, we must learn where wisdom *cannot* be found. In fact, there are two places where it cannot be retrieved.

First, wisdom cannot be discovered by human means. Job 28:1-11 is a poetic description of searching the depths of the earth. It's a description of what mankind has accomplished but still falls short in finding true wisdom.

> "Surely there is a mine for silver And a place where they refine gold. Iron is taken from the dust, And copper is smelted from rock. *Man* puts an end to darkness, And to the farthest limit he searches out The rock in gloom and deep shadow. He sinks a shaft far from habitation, Forgotten by the foot; They hang and swing to and fro far from men. The earth, from it comes food, And underneath it is turned up as fire. Its rocks are the source of sapphires, And its dust *contains* gold. The path no bird of prey knows, Nor has the falcon's eye caught sight of it. The proud beasts have not trodden it, Nor has the *fierce lion* passed over it. He puts his hand on the flint; He overturns the mountains at the base. He hews out channels through the rocks, And his eye sees anything precious. He dams up the streams from flowing, And what is hidden he brings out to the light."

Yet with all our collective advances in technology, medicine, and science in our enlightened, post-modern world, we can still ask what Job does in verse twelve: "'But where can wisdom be found? And where is the place of understanding?'" It's not discovered by human means.

Second, wisdom cannot be found by human money. Look at Job 28:15-19:

> "Pure gold cannot be given in exchange for [wisdom], Nor can silver be weighed as its price. It cannot be valued in the gold of Ophir, In precious onyx, or sapphire. Gold or glass cannot equal it, nor can it be exchanged for articles of fine gold. Coral and crystal are not to be mentioned; And the acquisition of wisdom is above *that of* pearls. The topaz of Ethiopia cannot equal it, Nor can it be valued in pure gold."

Job summarizes these questions in verse twenty: "'Where then does wisdom come from? And where is the place of understanding?'"

In contrast to these two ways, human means and human money, wisdom can be found in the Lord! Look at Job 28:23: "God understands [wisdom's] way, and He knows its place." God knows the place of wisdom because it is from Him. God is the Source of true wisdom in suffering. And so this is the key to knowing where we can find wisdom. We find wisdom in the fear of the Lord. Consider Job 28:28: "And to man He said, *'Behold, the fear of the Lord, that is wisdom; and to depart from evil is understanding'*" (emphasis added). Here is the main point: true wisdom in suffering can only be found in the fear of the Lord. And to understand this main point, we must understand what wisdom is and what the fear of the Lord is.

WHAT IS WISDOM?

J. I. Packer defines wisdom in this way: "Wisdom is the power to see, and the inclination to choose, the best and highest goal, together with the surest means of attaining it."[45] That definition is a mouthful, though. Wisdom, in simpler terms, is "knowledge applied to achieve the best." Let me give you an illustration that may help clarify this.

I was so excited to learn to drive. I got my license on the day I turned sixteen. But I was also nervous. I'll never forget pulling out of the parking lot of the DMV. I was so excited and so nervous that I thought I had put the car in reverse when I put it in drive. When I stepped on the gas a little too hard, I didn't pull out of the parking spot; I pulled right up onto the curb! Just so you know, that has never happened again! I learned a bit of wisdom from that experience.

I had read the books, taken the course, and passed the exams; but I had very little experience driving. Over time, I have learned the skill and have gained wisdom in driving. Wisdom knows when to yield, when to slam on the breaks, and when to step on the gas in each and every situation to achieve the best outcome. Now, of course, accidents still happen. My wisdom is not perfect. But wisdom gives you the ability to harness the knowledge that you have and apply it to life to achieve the best ends.

Wisdom in driving is one thing. In life and suffering, it is completely different. Wisdom, as it may seem from my car

---

45   J. I. Packer, *Knowing God* (Downers Grove: IVP, 1973), 90.

illustration, increases with age and experience. That is partly true but not entirely. Just because you're older does not mean that you are wiser. True wisdom that applies knowledge to a life of suffering only comes from the fear of the Lord. So what is the fear of the Lord?

WHAT IS THE FEAR OF THE LORD?

I've never quite understood the fear of the Lord until a few years ago. A teacher helped me to see the fear of the Lord by explaining two broad categories of fear.[46] In one sense, we all have what we could call "terror" fear. This is the feeling that is present when you are afraid of a situation or person that could harm you physically, financially, emotionally, or spiritually. Kids, for example, might have terror fear of their parent's discipline.

In another sense, there is fear that you might call "worship" fear. This kind of fear stands in awe and reverence of someone or something. You may experience this when standing at the edge of the Grand Canyon and find yourself in awe over the sheer magnitude of it.

Now that you have these two concepts of terror fear and worship fear in your mind, let me illustrate the difference between them to help you understand the fear of the Lord. What happens when you're driving down the highway and you run across a police car? If you're like me, your first instinct is to step

---

46   Edward T. Welch, *When People Are Big and God Is Small: Overcoming Peer Pressure, Codependency, and the Fear of Man* (Phillipsburg: P&R Publishing, 1997), 95-99.

on the break and check your speed. In a sense, you have *terror* fear of being pulled over and being issued a speeding violation. I've received a few in my life, and they are frightening, in a sense.[47]

Now what about "worship" fear? Let's say you are in a vessel faster than an automobile. Let's say you are in a rocket ship. When I watch NASA flights count down and takeoff, I always have a sense of "terror" just watching the takeoff, knowing that one little mistake will cost the astronauts their lives. I can't even imagine the "terror" the astronaut feels, no matter how much training he has had! But this "terror" very quickly disappears when the astronaut looks out his window and see the earth from miles above the surface. His "terror" fear turns into "worship" fear at the sight of such awesome sight of seeing the earth from outer space.

These two fears are two extremes on either end. This means there is a spectrum between the two. So you might move from terror to dread to trembling in a short period of time. After that, you may go from astonishment to awe to reverence. This, in turn, leads you to devotion, then to trust and worship.

Having said all this, here's where this hits home. If you are *not* a Christian, the fear of the Lord cannot really exist in a complete sense. The fear of God should cause *terror* in your heart because God is holy and righteous, and He will punish your sin for all eternity.

Although Christians also have terror fear in respect to the Lord, it leads them to worship fear. I like one author's definition of

---

47   Jim Berg, *Created for His Glory: God's Purpose for Redeeming Your Life* (Greenville: Bob Jones University Press, 2002), 219-220.

the fear of the Lord: "The fear of the Lord is the awe and reverence left over when the frightening vulnerability before the greatness of God is mixed with joy and security upon experiencing the goodness of God."[48] You could shorten this by saying the fear of God is the worship fear that replaces the terror fear. A person who fears the Lord trusts, loves, worships, and simply stands in awe of God above all else.

WHY IS WISDOM FOUND IN THE FEAR OF THE LORD?

Let's review what I have said about wisdom and the fear of the Lord. Wisdom is the application of knowledge to life. The fear of the Lord is the worship fear left over after the terror fear is gone. Now, we can answer an important question: why is the fear of the Lord wisdom?

The fear of the Lord is true wisdom because when you worship, honor, and love God above all else, you are simultaneously teachable and humble toward Him. That is the posture of your heart. And in this posture, you can receive wisdom. This is why Proverbs—a book all about wisdom—says that "with the humble is wisdom" (Prov. 11:2).

OBTAINING WISDOM IN SUFFERING

But you're not Job. So how do you get wisdom in suffering? I want you to think about all that is in your life that isn't sin but is suffering: cancer, disease, pain, trauma, inabilities, and

---

48   Berg, 216.

pressures. What do you do when life falls apart? What decisions should you make when faced with financial, physical, relational, or emotional suffering? We need wisdom in the face of suffering all the time. So how can you gain wisdom?

True wisdom starts with the fear of the Lord. It starts when your heart is so captivated and captured by God that your terror fear turns into worship fear. You are naturally driven to rely on yourself. You live for your own kingdom, a kingdom that is driven by all kinds of fears. Listen to what Paul Tripp says:

> The kingdom of self is driven by all kinds of other fears: fear of man, fear of discomfort or difficulty, fear of failure, fear of not getting my own way, etc. . . . The principle here is that if God doesn't own the fear of our hearts, He will not own our lives. You and I are always living to avoid what we dread. If we dread displeasing God more than anything else, because our hearts have been captured by a deep worshipful and loving awe of Him, we will live in new ways.[49]

What are these new ways of living? How can you receive wisdom? There are three ways:

First, you receive wisdom from God's Word. You live according to it—by faith not by sight. Psalm 19:7 reads, "The law of the LORD is perfect, restoring the soul; The testimony of the LORD is sure, making wise the simple." God's Word turns the

---

49   Paul David Tripp, *A Quest for Something More: Living for Something Bigger Than You* (Greensboro: New Growth Press, 2008), 127.

simple person into a wise person. Another verse which shows this is found in Psalm 119:98, which says, "Your commandments make me wiser than my enemies, For they are ever mine." God's commandments, a synonym for God's Word makes a person wise. This is why "[the] entire Bible," Ed Welch says, "is a textbook on the fear of the Lord."[50]

Second, not only does the fear of the Lord teach us to receive God's Word, but the fear of the Lord also causes us to *ask* for wisdom. This is exactly what James says in James 1:5: "But if any of you lacks wisdom, let him ask of God, who gives to all generously and without reproach, and it will be given to him." What I want to remind you about this great promise is that it is a promise to the person who is suffering—the person undergoing "various trials" as James put it (Jas. 1:2).

Third, wisdom is received from a relationship with Jesus Christ. The reality is that the search for wisdom is the search for a Person. Wisdom is not primarily a thing; it is a Person. Jesus is the Wisdom of God. Paul says that in Jesus Christ "are hidden all the treasures of wisdom and knowledge" (Col. 2:3). Jesus, infinitely more than Job, feared God and turned away from evil. As a Christian, Jesus has become to you, by God's doing, the wisdom from God (1 Cor. 1:30). So your search for wisdom in suffering is a search for God Himself. This is the fear of the Lord! It is the worship of Him above all. It is the satisfaction that when all is said and done, though no answers may be given to

---

50 Welch, 103.

why you are suffering and the pain has not been taken away, you say, "Blessed be the name of the LORD" (Job 1:21).

It is no surprise, then, what God says about Job in the very first chapter. Do you remember the words? God asks Satan if he has considered His servant Job, whom God says is "a blameless and upright man, fearing God and turning away from evil" (Job 1:8). How do I know Job feared God? When all was taken from him, he worshipped! "Then Job arose and tore his robe and shaved his head, and he fell to the ground and worshipped" (Job 1:20). Job never received answers as to why he was suffering. But he did receive God, and that's the point.

At the end of the day, the lesson we learn from the book of Job is not how to manage, escape, or heal from suffering. The lesson is that suffering is meant to lead us to a Person. True wisdom—the fear of the Lord—is to be content and satisfied and to worship God in the face of suffering, for He gives and takes away (Job 1:21).

CONCLUSION

I'll never forget the testimony of a man named John, which I heard at a church baptism. John was a traveling musician. As he went from one gig to another, drugs, alcohol, and women were a constant in John's life. Years of sin brought on years of suffering and pain. But when I saw John baptized, he said that the shortest poem in the English language is this: "Born, suffered, died." That pretty much sums up life.

But then John went on to say that the poem does not fit his life. The poem needed to change. The poem for his new life in Christ is now, "Born, suffered, *born again*." Christianity does not cancel out suffering. What Christianity does is give wisdom in suffering because, ultimately, Christianity gives us Jesus, the One Who suffered in our place.

CHAPTER 8

JUSTIFICATION AND SUFFERING

JOB 29:1-31:40

MANY YEARS AGO, I WAS called into a board room full of pastors. I didn't quite know why, but I had a hunch it wasn't good. About fifteen minutes into the conversation, I learned why I had come: they offered admonition for some areas of concern in my life. As I sat there, my heart beat a little faster; my face began to flush; and I began to rise to my own defense, initially in my heart and then with words. Have you ever been there? Can you relate? Has a pastor, spouse, parent, teacher, or friend corrected you in your tracks? I'm sure you've been there at least once in your life.

Why is it so hard to accept critique, criticism, and correction? Why is confrontation and rebuke hard, even when done in love? Why do we, as one person says, want to believe we are in the "good class" of sinners? Why do we find comfort in pointing out other people's faults to make ourselves look better? Why do we exaggerate the truth, leave out important details, or spin history to make ourselves look better than we are?[51] These are good questions, and they have a good answer! But first, we have to understand how this relates to the book of Job because he was right there.

JOB'S FINAL DEFENSE

Job had suffered a cataclysmic loss. On the heel of his life-changing suffering, Job's three "friends" sat down with him to have "the talk." From Job's perspective, the conversation went south . . . fast. His friends essentially argued that Job was suffering because he sinned in a particular way, so he's getting what he deserves (Job 18).

Like you and I want to do, Job rises to his own defense. His closing arguments are contained in chapters twenty-nine through thirty-one. Though these chapters are not the only time Job defends his righteousness, it will be his last. We've examined the friends' arguments, but how does Job respond to them?

CHAPTER 29: JUSTIFICATION IN THE PAST

To begin with, in chapter twenty-nine, Job justifies himself by speaking about his relationship with God and then his relationship with others. As any believer would, Job recalls his good relationship with God. Here's how he describes his relationship with the Lord. Look with me at Job 29:2-6:

---

51   Adapted from Paul David Tripp, *Whiter Than Snow: Meditations on Sin and Mercy* (Wheaton: Crossway, 2008), 27-28.

"Oh that I were as in months gone by, As in the days when God watched over me; When His lamp shone over my head, *And* by His light I walked through darkness; As I was in the prime of my days, When the friendship of God *was* over my tent; when the Almighty was yet with me, *And* my children were around me; When my steps were bathed in butter, And the rock poured out for me streams of oil!"

This is all poetic language to say, "I had a good relationship with God." Not only that, but Job also had a good relationship with other people. Look with me at some of his words in Job 29:7-20:

"When I went out to the gate of the city, When I took my seat in the square, The young men saw me and hid themselves, And the old men arose *and* stood. The princes stopped talking And put *their* hands on their mouths; The voice of the nobles was hushed, And their tongue stuck to their palate. For when the ear heard, it called me blessed, And when the eye saw, it gave witness of me, Because I delivered the poor who cried for help, And the orphan who had no helper. The blessing of the one ready to perish came upon me, And I made the widow's heart sing for joy. I put on righteousness, and it clothed me; My justice was like a robe and a turban. I was eyes to the blind And feet to the lame. I was a father to the needy, And I investigated the case which I did not know. I broke the jaws of the wicked And snatched the prey from his teeth. Then I thought, 'I shall die in my nest, And I shall multiply *my* days as the sand.

> My root is spread out to the waters, And dew lies all
> night on my branch. My glory is *ever* new with me,
> And my bow is renewed in my hand.'"

In other words, Job is not only a powerful and wealthy man, but he is also a generous man. There is a stereotype that wealthy people are uncaring, insensitive, and out of touch—but not Job. He really did care about people—so much so that Francis Andersen points out that Job's care for the poor, fatherless, and marginalized was a model for how Old Testament ethics were supposed to be. "In Job's conscience," the commentator says, "to omit to do good to any fellow human being, of whatever rank or class, would be a grievous offense to God."[52] Job was a good guy. Yet he suffered. Job doesn't doubt that the bad guy suffers, but Job is making the case that he is the good guy; he is innocent and righteous.

CHAPTER 30: JUSTIFICATION IN THE PRESENT

Job 30, however, turns rather abruptly. It reminds me that a person undergoing severe and intense suffering can quickly vacillate from highs to lows. Chapter thirty is like a more intense version of chapter three because it is a lament about Job's suffering. However, while Job is grieving, he does so with an eye to defending his own righteousness. After many bitter words, he says in Job 30:24-25, "Yet does not one in a heap of ruins stretch out *his* hand, Or in his disaster therefore

---

52 Anderson, 231.

cry out for help? Have I not wept for the one whose life is hard? Was not my soul grieved for the needy?"

The argument is this: look at all that I've done for others. I am innocent. I do not deserve this pain. I have pain just reading about Job's pain! What anguish of soul he is in!

CHAPTER 31: JUSTIFICATION IN ALL OF LIFE

Finally, in chapter thirty-one, Job offers his closing remarks. I find chapter thirty-one so interesting because it assumes a pattern. Job lists a sin, the judgment for that sin, the reason for the judgment, and then declares he is innocent of the sin. Like a lawyer arguing his case, Job makes his best case. Here is a list of sins he exonerates himself of:[53]

- Lust (vv. 1-4)
- Dishonesty (vv. 5-8)
- Adultery (vv. 9-12)
- Injustice to the weak (vv. 13-15)
- Stinginess (vv. 16-23)
- Greed or trust in wealth (vv. 24-25)
- Idolatry (vv. 26-28)
- Vindictiveness (vv. 29-30)
- Not showing hospitality or generosity (vv. 31-32)
- Hypocrisy (vv. 33-34)
- Exploitation (vv. 38-40)

---

53   Lists adapted from Ash, 311-318.

"None of it," Job says. "I have done none of these things." So, listen to Job's final challenge in Job 31:35-37: "Oh that I had one to hear me! Behold, here is my signature; Let the Almighty answer me! And the indictment which my adversary has written, Surely I would carry it on my shoulder, I would bind it to myself like a crown. I would declare to Him the number of my steps; Like a prince I would approach Him."

Thus, after eighteen chapters of speech in the book, Job ends his speech and only says a few more words in the remainder of the book. In chapters twenty-nine through thirty-one, Job argues that he is innocent; he has done nothing wrong. Here is a man, from Job's own perspective, who has done nothing to deserve the suffering he is experiencing. But is he right in this assessment? And what lesson can be learned for us in suffering?

RETRIBUTION SUFFERING[54]

It seems, in one sense, Job was right to defend and declare his innocence. Certainly, Job was a sinner—we know that from the rest of Scripture. But the book of Job gives us no inside scoop into a specific sin that is tied to his suffering. In the very beginning of the book, the narrator says he is blameless (Job 1:8); and at the very end of the book, God says Job has spoken rightly about God (Job 42:7). Remember, however, this is what *we* know from the narration of the book. As far as Job knew, he had to defend

---

54   I was helped on some of these thoughts by: Tchividjian, *Glorious Ruin*, chapter four.

himself. This is precisely what Job could not understand. He was ready to admit his sin if he had sinned. But to him, he had not done anything wrong. It felt to Job like God was punishing him.

"God," said Job, "if I have done something wrong, punish me. But I don't believe I have. So why am I suffering so much? I am innocent."

In saying this, Job betrays that his theology of suffering was no better than his friends. It is still based on retribution. This is just a fancy word for saying that if you do right, you will be blessed; but if you do wrong, you will be cursed. This sort of mindset is not unique to Job, his friends, or the Ancient Near East. It is deeply ingrained in all of us. The way we commonly think is that good people get good stuff, and bad people get bad stuff.

The lab results come back positive, so you think it is punishment. Your marriage goes south, and you believe God is getting back at you for your sinful choices. Or, consider this, how do you think of the poor, fatherless, and marginalized? Do you say to yourself, "They have made their own bed; they must sleep in it! Besides, this is America, they can get out of poverty if they want to?" I'm not offering any kind of political or social critique. My point is that in our own lives and culture, the good people get good stuff and the bad people get bad stuff. To clarify, I'm not denying consequences for actions, but not everything can be chalked up to a "this-for-that" kind of schema.

A while back, a former colleague was descending church stairs, missed the bottom step, and fractured her ankle in the process. As customers entered and saw her in crutches, I can't tell you how many said—in a half-joking way that was, nonetheless, serious—"You must have upset God, especially since you injured yourself at church!" Had my co-worker sinned to deserve a fractured ankle?

That is exactly the mentality of Job's friends, and it became Job's mindset. They believed Job had sinned and upset God, so he was suffering the consequences of his behavior. In other words, Job was a bad actor. However, Job didn't dispute their theology. He simply sought to defend himself.

JUSTIFICATION AND SUFFERING

In one sense, we can say Job had not sinned in a specific way to merit the suffering. But in another sense, he *is* a sinner who needs justification. This is why justification is so important, whether our suffering is the result of a specific sin or not. Job desperately wanted justification, and so do we.

This is a challenging enigma Job finds himself in. He is accused of sin and arguing for his innocence, yet he is really a sinner. We cannot truly understand any of this apart from what later revelation, the New Testament, will call the doctrine of justification.

The doctrine of justification is the truth that you and I have broken God's righteous, holy laws. You are guilty and deserve condemnation for your sins. But because of God's great love, grace, and mercy, He sent Christ Jesus as an atonement for your sins. On the cross, Christ accomplished your salvation. And so, it is through turning from yourself and turning to Christ that your sins are wiped away. You become justified. That is, you are declared and defended as forgiven of all your sins. Christ gets all your sin. What's more, you get all His righteousness. Your spiritual bank account goes from negative billions to positive billions, not negative billions to zero. This is truly how Job could defend and declare his innocence. But what does Job have to do with the doctrine of justification?

I once heard an Old Testament professor say that the Old Testament is where it's at; the rest is just commentary. If that is the case, the commentary on Job is undoubtedly Hebrews 11:1-2: "Now faith is the assurance of *things* hoped for, the conviction of things not seen. For by it the men of old gained approval." *Approval* is a word for righteousness or justification. Job was justified by his faith!

The book of Job points forward with simple faith to the finished work of Christ. This is how you and I gain approval with God. Job looked forward to Christ, and we look backward to Christ. Whatever limited revelation Job had, his trust in God was credited as righteousness. In this sense, Job was indeed righteous.

LOOK TO CHRIST IN YOUR SUFFERING FOR JUSTIFICATION

What does this mean for you and me? What lesson can we learn from the book of wisdom on suffering? In your suffering—trials, tribulations, heartache, and pain—keep your focus on the Sufferer, Jesus Christ, Who suffered for your justification. Suffering causes you and me to turn our focus inward. We question why. What did we do to deserve the pain? And when we truly and honestly look inside, we must admit that we are fundamentally guilty.

But looking inward will lead you to the path of despair or self-righteousness, which will compile your pain. Looking to Christ, however, Who is your righteousness, will give you the spiritual standing to endure the pain. This word "standing" connects to a beautiful passage on suffering in Romans 5:1-2, which says, "Therefore, having been justified by faith, we have peace with God through our Lord Jesus Christ, through whom also we have obtained our introduction by faith into this grace in which we stand; and we exult in hope of the glory of God." The connection to suffering can be found in the very next verse, "And not only this, but we also exult in our tribulation, knowing that tribulation brings about perseverance."

What does justification have to do with suffering? A whole lot! Romans 5:1 and its following verses deal with the *results* of justification. What are those results? It starts with peace but doesn't end there. Justification gives you a perspective on suffering that gives so much hope that you *exult* in your sufferings. Instead of despising or running from your suffering, you can rejoice in suffering. We can look at ourselves in the mirror and know that Jesus has paid our debt.

Yes, I still suffer, but I have the exulting "hope of the glory of God." I no longer seek to justify myself to myself or before the eyes of people, even if I am falsely accused; but I look to Christ in my suffering for my justification of all my wrongs.

CONCLUSION

I don't know all the intricate details of the suffering you are going through as you read this book, but here is what the Lord is saying to you. When you suffer, in your heart and mind, don't look inside yourself. Look outside yourself to Christ. As I alluded to in the beginning of the chapter, every one of us seeks to justify ourselves. No one wants to be accused of wrong. No one especially wants to be falsely accused of wrong. But you are justified, believer. You are righteous in God's eyes, no matter what the accusations may be.

So, in the deep resources of your soul and heart, in your naked and bare conscience before your Maker, no matter who accuses you of wrong—whether it is the devil, your own self, or someone else—admit your sin where you have sinned. Look outward to Jesus Christ in your suffering. Look at His finished work. Look to Him for justification and defense.

CHAPTER 9
JUSTICE AND SUFFERING

JOB 32:1-37:24

DAVID JACKSON, PROFESSOR AND AUTHOR of a popular commentary on the book of Job, wrote this while going through an intense period of suffering:

> I discovered Job when I was sitting by my wife's hospital bed, waiting for her to wake up after a miscarriage. We had prayed for this child's safety and salvation since before the child was conceived. We had prayed all that night that the child would survive the present crisis. The answer was no. I sat there, looking out the window of the hospital at sunrise, and watched a bird fly across a cloudless sky as the sun rose. I asked the Lord, "How come that wretched bird could soar through such a sunrise, and our child, made in your image, never saw the light of day?"[55]

If I could summarize what Jackson was feeling in three words, it would be this: "That's not fair." How many times

---

55   Jackson, 1.

have we spoken or thought these words? If we are truthful, it is often. There is perhaps much in life that isn't fair. Some people even live in a "that's not fair" attitude for much of their lives:

- It's not fair that we lost the game because the referee made a really bad call.
- It's not fair that I am not as smart, beautiful, or talented as my sibling.
- It's not fair that the rich prosper while I don't.
- It's not fair that some children are born with cancer.

Of course, it's easy to say to our kids when they get a smaller slice of cake, "Life isn't fair; and the sooner you figure that out, the happier you'll be!" Yet as true as that may be, deep down inside, you have a sense of right and wrong; you have a sense of justice. Everyone does.

What we see in the book of Job is a divinely inspired account of the intersection between justice and suffering. In a very real way, justice is at the heart of the book of Job. Job feels that God has been unjust to him because he is suffering without cause. Job's friends feel like God is being completely just to punish Job with suffering because they believe Job sinned. And Elihu—a new character who shows up in these last chapters—believes Job is unjustly misrepresenting God. Yes, justice, in many ways, is at the heart of the book of Job.

I want to look at the words of Elihu. He is concerned with justice—especially the justice of God—more than any other character in the book of Job. His speeches take up chapters thirty-two through thirty-seven. And in looking at Elihu's words, we can continue to see what wisdom lessons we can learn from the book of Job, as it relates to justice and suffering.

ELIHU'S ANGER

Elihu is angry. Anger is repeated four times in four verses. Look at Job 32:2-5:

> But the *anger* of Elihu the son of Barachel the Buzite, of the family of Ram burned; against Job his *anger* burned because he justified himself before God. And his *anger* burned against his three friends because they had found no answer, and yet had condemned Job. Now Elihu had waited to speak to Job because they were years older than he. And when Elihu saw that there was no answer in the mouth of the three men his *anger* burned (emphasis added).

Elihu is angry because he believes God has been misrepresented as being unjust. He is chiefly concerned with God's justice.[56] And therefore, Elihu's perspective is not the

---

56 I see Elihu as a positive character who contributes something new to the conversation because what he speaks about God which aligns with the rest of Scripture, and God never rebukes Elihu (see Job 42:7-8). Others see Elihu as a negative character who doesn't contribute anything new to the conversation (Eric Ortlund, *Suffering Wisely & Well: The Grief of Job and the Grace of God* [Wheaton: Crossway, 2022], 83-84).

same as that of Job's other friends. Here is how it is different according to the commentator Hywel Jones: "[The friends] said that Job was suffering because he had sinned. Elihu says that Job has sinned because he was suffering."[57] Do you see the difference? The friends say Job is suffering because of his sin. Elihu says Job sinned—misrepresented God—because he is suffering. Thus, Elihu rebukes Job with two basic arguments that will lead to three wisdom lessons.

ELIHU'S FIRST ARGUMENT: THOUGH GOD IS NOT OBLIGATED TO ANSWER, HE HAS SPOKEN

First, Elihu rebukes Job for portraying God as silent in his suffering (Job 23:3, 8-9). This argument has two parts—that God is not obligated to answer Job and that God has indeed already answered Job.

Elihu responds to Job by saying that God is not obligated to answer anyone in their suffering. God is not subject to human reasoning and explanation. God owes no one an answer. Look at Elihu's rebuke in Job 33:12-13: "Behold, let me tell you, you are not right in this, For God is greater than man. Why do you complain against Him That He does not give an account of all His doings?" The implication is clear. God does not owe Job any explanation or apology. But God has already spoken, as we will see below.

---

57   Hywel R. Jones, *Job* (Darlington: Evangelical Press, 2007), 226.

ELIHU'S SECOND ARGUMENT: GOD MUST BE JUST

The second main argument that Elihu brings to the table is to confront Job's insistence that God must be unjust. Job thinks he is suffering unjustly because of his belief that only the unrighteous suffer. Job, however, has argued at great lengths that he is righteous and doesn't deserve what he is going through. In fact, Elihu summarizes Job's arguments like this in Job 34:5-6: "For Job has said, 'I am righteous, But God has taken away my right; Should I lie concerning my right? My wound is incurable, thought I am without transgression.'"

To rebut Job's misrepresentation of God, Elihu argues that God is just in His character and therefore just in His actions. Look at his words in Job 34:12: "Surely God will not act wickedly, And the Almighty will not pervert justice." Elihu masterfully vindicates God's justice.

LESSON 1: GOD DOES NOT OWE YOU AN EXPLANATION FOR YOUR SUFFERING

We all need to be rebuked at times. That is, we all need to have our thinking in alignment with God's Word and ways. So often in your suffering, you want to know why. But God is Sovereign over all the suffering in your life. This means that He is in control. It also means that He has a right to do what He wants to do that fits His purposes.

But let me make something clear—it is not wrong to ask why. Many people in the Scriptures ask that question. Christ certainly asked why in His suffering. Remember His heart-wrenching words on the cross? "MY GOD, MY GOD, WHY HAVE YOUR FORSAKEN ME" (Matt. 27:46)? It's not wrong to ask why. It's wrong when you demand God to speak and require Him to give you a reason. How do you know when you are doing this? You become angry at God. You let yourself turn bitter against Him.

Have you ever been there? If we're honest, we all have. But as Martin Luther wisely reminds us: "We should remember the lesson that Job learned: no one can summon God into court to account for what He does or allows to happen."[58]

But a second lesson also shapes our view and understanding of justice and suffering.

LESSON 2: GOD SPEAKS IN YOUR SUFFERING, IF ONLY YOU HAVE EARS TO HEAR

I want you to notice that Elihu goes a step further after rebuking Job by saying that God does not owe him an explanation or answer. He also rebukes Job for failing to hear God, for God has already spoken. God has not remained silent. Look what Elihu says in Job 33:14: "Indeed, God speaks once, or twice, *yet* no one notices it." Did you hear that (pun intended)?

There are basically three ways that Elihu tells Job that God has already spoken in his suffering. God speaks through dreams

---

58   Martin Luther, *Faith Alone: A Daily Devotional*, ed. James C. Galvin (Grand Rapids: Zondervan, 1998, 2005), 5020. Kindle.

and visions (Job 33:15-16); He speaks through suffering itself (Job 33:19); and He speaks through angels and people (Job 33:23-24). We're not Old Testament people, so what does this mean for us? God speaks to you in your suffering in three ways.

First, God speaks to you in your suffering through His Word. I don't only mean the Scriptures. God also speaks to you through the Word—the Lord Jesus Christ. Remember the opening words of the book of Hebrews: "God, after He spoke long ago to the fathers in the prophets in many portions and in many ways, in these last days has spoken to us in His Son" (Heb. 1:1-2a). God's final revelation is Jesus Christ and the Scriptures. This is His Word to you in your suffering. The book of Job was written to give you wisdom in your suffering.

Second, God speaks to you in your suffering through other people. "And He gave some *as* apostles, and some *as* prophets, and some *as* evangelists, and some *as* pastors and teachers for the equipping of the saints, for the work of service, to the building up of the body of Christ" (Eph. 4:11-12). God has given fellow believers who speak to one another "with all wisdom teaching and admonishing one another" (Col. 3:16) and "[to speak] the truth in love" (Eph. 4:15). God "comforts us in all our affliction so that we will be able to comfort those who are in any affliction with the comfort with which we ourselves are comforted by God" (2 Cor. 1:4). God speaks to you through the Church—the people of God, as they apply the Word to your life through preaching, counseling, and discipleship.

Third, God speaks to you through the suffering itself. C. S. Lewis once said in his book, *The Problem of Pain*, "God whispers to us in our pleasures, speaks in our conscience, but shouts in our pain: it is His megaphone to rouse a deaf world."[59] Suffering, Lewis says, gets your attention. When you suffer, that's when you seek answers and find God. It's not during the good times. When you experience pain, hardship, difficulty, and suffering, it puts you in a position to be receptive to what God has to say through His Word and through His people. God is not silent. He has spoken in your suffering. Listen for His voice in these three ways.

LESSON 3: GOD IS JUST IN ALL THE SUFFERING IN YOUR LIFE

We already saw that God is Sovereign over all the suffering of your life. But as the old "problem of evil" would have it, God may be all-powerful; but He cannot be completely just and good at the same time. However, this isn't a problem for the Bible! The Scripture presents a God Who is simultaneously powerful, good, wise, and just in every part of your suffering. Think about it. If He were just but not powerful, how would we have any hope that justice could prevail in the universe? Or if He were all powerful but not just, how cruel and horrible the universe would be—a zillion times worse than it is.[60]

---

59   C. S. Lewis, *The Problem of Pain*, in *The Complete C. S. Lewis Signature Classics* (San Francisco: Harper One, 1940, 2002), 604.
60   Wayne Grudem, *Systematic Theology* (Grand Rapids: Zondervan, 1994), 205.

Even more importantly, why does this matter? This matters a great deal because of how I began. We are hardwired to want justice. We all have a built-in sense of right and wrong. Not one of us had to teach our kids about justice. They instinctively know what it is when a toy is ripped from their hands. Anger, like Elihu demonstrated, is an emotion we experience when perceived injustice happens.

Therefore, it is no wonder that our culture is starving for justice. I listened to some of the Senate hearings for the Supreme Court Justice, Ketanji Brown Jackson. They asked many questions of her to determine if she would be "just" in her decisions. Take one hot button issue: abortion. One side argues that it's not fair for the unborn to have no voice. The other side argues that it's not fair for a woman to have no voice. One side wants the right to life; the other side wants the right to abortion. The point is that each side wants rights; each side wants justice, whatever their respective standard of justice is. We could multiply examples.

But let's not think about the world "out there." Let's think about your own life and the suffering in your own life. Why has God allowed the strife, turmoil, heartache, and pain? And since He has, does this mean He is not just?

My answer to this challenging question is the answer Elihu gives Job. We may never know why. From a human perspective, life does not always add up the way it should. But God's ways are higher than our ways (Isa. 55:8-9). Here is how Elihu put this to Job in Job 35:2, "'Do you think this is according to justice? Do you say, *My righteousness is more than God's?'"* (emphasis added). You can't claim this. Are you more just than God? In fact, all you can assert is that you are unrighteous. You have committed acts of injustice in this life. It's called sin. Conversely, God is the definition of justice because you deserve to die and suffer eternally for your sin, but God sent His only Son Jesus to suffer in your place. God, you see, is just. And not only that, but He is also the Justifier of the one who has faith in Jesus (Rom. 3:26). Here's how Elihu puts it in Job 37:23: "'The Almighty—we cannot find Him; He is exalted in power And He will not do violence to justice and abundant righteousness."

Here is the takeaway: put your trust and hope in Jesus. Put it in the One Who is completely just, as Peter writes (1 Pet. 2:22-23). Peter says that we may suffer in this life, even suffer unjustly. But it's not those who suffer for doing wrong that are blessed, but those who suffer for doing right in the face of injustice (1 Pet. 1:20). In the face of unjust suffering, the answer, Peter says, is to follow Jesus Who "entrusted *Himself* to Him who judges righteously" (1 Pet 2:23). As John Calvin said beautifully, "We do not always see justice in this life, but as long as we cling by faith to God's justice, we can pour into His bosom the difficulties which torment us, in order that He may loosen the knots that we cannot untie."[61] This doesn't mean we abandon the legal system and "leave it all to God." It means we

---

61 Calvin, *Commentaries*, quoted in Joel R. Beeke and Paul M. Smalley, *Reformed Systematic Theology, Vol 1, Revelation and God* (Wheaton: Crossway, 2019), 812.

fight for justice as much as we can. And when all is said and done, we trust God to "loosen the knots that we cannot untie."

CONCLUSION

I began the chapter with the testimony of David Jackson, a man who suffered the loss of his child. I want to conclude the chapter with the remainder of his testimony, because it is spot on with the message of the chapter. After asking the Lord "why" and saying in his heart, "That's not fair," he says:

> I opened my Bible to Job because I figured he might have something to say at a time [of deep suffering], and I flipped through the pages to roughly the end of the book. I was looking for God's final speech to Job. My eye fell on the questions, "Where were you when I laid the earth's foundations . . . Have you ever given orders to the morning, or show the dawn its place . . . Do you know when the mountain goats give birth . . . Does the hawk take flight by your wisdom?"[62]

Then Jackson continues, "I sat and wept and remembered Job's words, 'Naked I came from my mother's womb, and naked I will depart. The Lord gave and the Lord has taken away; may the name of the Lord be praised.'"[63] God is just, though we do not understand all his ways, especially his ways of suffering. So, like Job, we trust and rest our case ultimately in the hands of God.

---

62 Jackson, 1-2.
63 Jackson, 2.

CHAPTER 10

GOD AND SUFFERING

JOB 38:1-42:6

I'M NOT A SOCIAL MEDIA person. I have a hard enough time keeping up with my life in the real world, let alone the social media world. I find the interaction on social media to be generally unhelpful. Twitter (or X), for example, allows a limited number of characters. It's extremely difficult to carry on a meaningful conversation with a limited number of characters. At the same time, on rare occasions, a complex topic or idea is summarized succinctly with 280 characters or less. One tweet summarized the book of Job well: "Job in a nutshell: Job: Why? Friends: You sinned. Job: No I didn't. God: Look at all the cool animals!"[64]

After thirty-seven chapters of arguing and complaining about why Job is suffering, the Lord breaks forth out of the whirlwind (Job 38:1) and speaks directly to Job—two times, in

---

64 Tony Reinke, "The Secrets of God in Our Suffering: Trusting Him with Unanswered Questions," *Desiring God* (blog), February 27, 2016, https://www.desiringgod.org/articles/the-secrets-of-god-in-our-suffering.

fact. God is gracious with Job; He allows Job to have a voice, something sufferers desperately long for. In this sense, Job gets what he asked for: a hearing with God. There is much wisdom we can learn from these chapters. What I want to do is discover three wisdom lessons we learn from God's speeches.

LESSON 1: SUFFERING DRAWS YOU INTO YOURSELF

Job thinks he knows how the world should be run: be good, and you'll be blessed; be bad, and you'll be cursed. This is the formula that Job clings to; this is the theology that Job believes. But Job's world does not turn out this way. Life is not what he expected, and he could not understand why. Have you ever been there? Life doesn't turn out the way you expect because suffering gets in the way—an illness, accident, financial loss, relationship loss, or death.

That's part of the problem with suffering. It may not be only physical pain, even though that's bad enough. It may be the fact that things don't add up, life isn't fair, justice hasn't been served, or it all doesn't turn out the way you planned. What happens when your parent is diagnosed with mental illness? What happens when you unexpectedly get laid off from a successful job? Suffering, which none of us want or welcome, changes our lives. Sometimes, the agony is small; sometimes, it is big and life-altering, like terminal cancer or mental illness. But pain is never what we want. No one buys the hardship tickets. No one wants to attend the affliction concert.

With all this said, what suffering does to you is pull you into yourself. Suffering drags you into your own little world. You feel sorry for yourself. You complain. You grumble. You mope. You want other people to feel sorry for you, and your whole view of reality becomes distorted.

The problem with suffering is what it does to you. I've made it clear that suffering is not necessarily the direct result of a specific sin. It was not for Job. Job was an innocent sufferer. And yet the problem was that because of his suffering, he began to be drawn into his own little world. Because of his suffering, he distorted God and reality. Anthony Selvaggio explains this well when he says, "Job is not confessing a sin that was a cause of his suffering,[sic] rather he is confessing a sin that resulted from his suffering."[65]

This is where God's first speech to Job is so helpful. God's speech draws Job out of himself. Job went inward; God drew him out. How does God draw Job out of himself? God draws Job out of himself by blowing his mind away with the bigness, power, and extravagance of the creation. Let's look more closely at two examples God gives.

God exerts absolute control over the heavenly constellations. Look at Job 38:31-33 and notice God's power and control. "Can you bind the chains of the Pleiades, Or loose the cords of Orion? Can you lead forth a constellation in its season, And guide the Bear with her satellites? Do you know the ordinances of the heavens,

---

65   Selvaggio, 144.

Or fix their rule over the earth?" Commentators are unsure what it means to "bind," "loose," and "guide" these heavenly objects. But however you take these words, God is ruling and controlling, not Job! God is taking Job outside of himself. God is saying, "I got this. I'm in control, even over your suffering. "

But it's not only inanimate creation God controls; it is the animal creation as well. I love the description of the ostriches in Job 39:13-18. Look at it with me.

> The ostriches' wings flap joyously with the pinion and plumage of love, For she abandons her eggs to the earth And warms them in the dust, And she forgets that a foot may crush them, Or that a wild beast may trample them. She treats her young cruelly, as if *they* were not hers; Though her labor be in vain, *she* is unconcerned; Because God has made her forget wisdom, And has not given her a share of understanding. When she lifts herself on high, She laughs at the horse and his rider.

This description is quite hilarious. It says that God has made the ostriches stupid! Look what she does. She lays her eggs and then abandons them (Job 39:14). "She forgets that a foot may crush them" (Job 39:15). Indeed, "[she] treats her young cruelly, as if *they* were not hers" (Job 39:16). Who gives birth and leaves their offspring on the side of the road? And yet, it is God Who had made her stupid (Job 39:17). God is in complete control of all of it, from stars in the sky to the dumb ostrich on earth. So, in essence, God tells Job in the first speech, "I have made no mistake, Job. I know exactly what I am doing. My plans and My counsel are perfect."

And Job is humbled. Look at his first response in Job 40:3-5: "Then Job answered the LORD and said, 'Behold, I am insignificant; what can I reply to You? I lay my hand on my mouth. Once I have spoken, and I will not answer; even twice, and I will add nothing more.'" Job finally admits that there is much more happening in the world than he knows. "Therefore, I have declared that which I do not understand, Things too wonderful for me, which I did not know" (Job 42:3b). Job doesn't know half of it. And so, he puts his hand over his mouth in silence (Job 40:4).

This is how God works. As I once heard, God must break you before He can make you. There is much you and I don't know in our suffering. Suffering humbles us, so we can see outside of ourselves how things really are. Pride is the result of turning inward. Humility is the result of turning outward. This leads us to the second lesson found in these chapters.

LESSON 2: GOD IS GOOD—EVEN IN YOUR SUFFERING

During suffering, in those moments when you're looking outward to God—though they may be rare—you know God is all-powerful. But you tell yourself, "God isn't good. How can a good God allow this to happen to me?" This is where Job finds himself. How is it good that God allows all Job's children to be killed before letting Job go bankrupt and writhe in pain from the puss that oozed of out of his skin? All for what? To teach Job a lesson? To prove Satan wrong? Certainly, there must have been an easier way!

Job questioned God's justice, which means he questioned God's goodness. To question one of these attributes is to also question the other. They are connected because, as Irenaeus says, "Justice without goodness is not just, and goodness without justice is not good, so the true God must be both good and just."[66] In fact, to doubt one of God's attributes is to doubt all of God's attributes. You can't question one thing about Him—like, if He really loves you—and not be questioning other things about Him, like His justice and sovereignty. This is how God describes Job's accusation in Job 40:6-8: "Then the LORD answered Job out of the storm and said, 'Now gird up your loins like a man; I will ask you, and you instruct Me. Will you really annul My judgment? Will you condemn Me that you may be justified?'"

God's response to Job demonstrates His goodness. God is saying, "Job, I am good to all My creation." Chapters 38-41 are literally dripping with God's goodness. Look what God does for the desert land in Job 38:25-27: "'Who has cleft a channel for the flood, Or a way for the thunderbolt, To bring rain on a land without people, *On* a desert without a man in it. To satisfy the waste and desolate land, And to make the seeds of grass to sprout?'" We take the rain for granted. But when you live in the desert, rain is a precious demonstration of the goodness of God.

---

66   Irenaeus, quoted in Beeke and Smalley, 811.

God even feeds the lions and the ravens. Check out Job 38:39-41: "Can you hunt the prey for the lion, Or satisfy the appetite of the young lions, When they crouch in *their* dens *And* lie in wait in *their* lair? Who prepares for the raven its nourishment when its young cry to God And wander about without food?"

In essence, God's logic to Job is that He has a good reason to ordain all things. Suffering came to pass in Job's life. Therefore, there was a good reason for the suffering of this righteous man.[67] But Job doesn't see it. He is wrapped up in himself until God comes to him in the whirlwind. Then Job learns. He is humbled when the Lord gives him the last lesson.

The last lesson flows from the first two. Because suffering draws you into yourself, in which you don't know the half of what God is up to, and God rules the world in goodness, there is a third and final lesson we can take away from God's speech.

LESSON 3: YOUR FUNDAMENTAL NEED IN YOUR SUFFERING IS GOD

The question which must be asked is did God answer Job's question? Job wanted an explanation for his suffering. Did God answer him? Yes and no. No, in the sense of, "Let Me tell you what happened, Job, what conversations took place in the heavenly vision. Let explain Myself to you, Job."[68] That's not how God responded. But, yes, God did answer Job because Job

---

67 Selvaggio, 148.
68 Selvaggio, 147.

responds with silence and repentance. Job does not say, "But I still don't understand. Explain Yourself to me." Job gets the point, and his question is satisfied. As one pastor says, for Job and often with us, "God is not willing to give us the answers that we want, but He does provide us with answers."[69]

Here is the answer that you need in your suffering. You don't essentially need relief from the pain. You don't necessarily need a fix for the problem or a plan for avoiding future suffering. You don't primarily even need an explanation of why you are suffering. What you and I need is a clearer, bigger, renewed vision of God. This is what Job meant when he said in Job 42:5, "I have heard of You by the hearing of the ear; But now my eye sees You." Job didn't have a literal vision with his physical eyes. It was as God was speaking words that the Ruler of the Universe revealed Himself to Job in all His glory, majesty, and splendor. He opened the eyes of Job's heart.

"What Job finally saw clearly is that he could not see clearly," writes one commentator.[70] Job missed it. Yes, Job was a believer. Yes, Job was a God-worshipper, giver, and server. Yes, Job lived a life of integrity. Yes, Job worked hard and was a good steward with his money. Job checked all the religious boxes, all the do's and don'ts we associate with biblical Christianity. Yet Job missed something. His suffering took him inside himself. Job needed

---

69   Selvaggio, 151.
70   O'Donnell, 112.

to look outside himself and "see God" for Who He really is. He needed a fresh, beautiful, big vision of God. I love what the late R. C. Sproul says: "Ultimately, the only answer God gave to Job was a revelation of Himself. It was as if God said to him, 'Job, *I* am your answer.' Job was not asked to trust a plan but a person, a personal God who is sovereign, wise, and good. It was as if God said to Job: 'Learn who I am. When you know Me, you know enough to handle everything.'"[71]

That's so true! We need to learn and know God, not just about Him. This was Paul's ambition! (Phil. 3:10). It's the difference between *knowing* the chemicals that make up honey and *tasting* honey. We need to know Him in an experiential way.[72] I'll put it like this—in your suffering, you need to see! It's not like everything will magically make sense. Job still didn't understand everything, but he saw enough of God for his heart to be settled.

You don't have to suffer to the extent of Job. Even before suffering strikes, you can possess a big, beautiful vision of God. You attend church where the preacher heralds the glories of Christ. You read the Bible where you encounter an all-satisfying Savior. And you can beg God, like Moses, to "show me Your glory" (Exod. 33:18). Only when you see God for Who He truly

---

71   R. C. Sproul, Surprised by *Suffering: The Role of Pain and Death in the Christian Life* (Orlando: Reformation Trust, 1988, 2009), 400. Kindle.

72   Dane Ortlund, *Deeper: Real Change for Real Sinners* (Wheaton: Crossway, 2021), 72. Kindle.

is and recognize how powerful, wise, just, and good He is, can you come to a place where you can trust Him. You don't trust someone who is a stranger to you, and you can't trust God when you doubt His attributes.

Yes, we trust other people. The irony, however, is that people will always fail you. People will always disappoint you. But God never will. When you find yourself longing for satisfaction, meaning, value, and purpose, you must turn your gaze outward toward God, not other people. True and lasting fulfillment is not found in a career, wealth, spouse, family, health, body image, or anything else. Everything else is but a "[broken cistern] that can hold no water" (Jer. 2:13).

The more you "see Him" for Who He really is, the more you can be like Him, John says (1 John 3:2). And the more you "see Him," the more you trust Him. Therefore, what you think of God is so important in your suffering. How you see God is critical to how you cope with your pain. So, will you trust God when it hurts? Will you trust God when the pain won't go away?

In the end, Job chose to trust God through the suffering. This is how Job began in the first chapter. But somewhere along the way, he got off course. However, he finally comes to his senses at the end when God patiently waits and then speaks!

What about you? Where are you at in your suffering? Have you lost sight of God? Have you taken your eyes off Him? He is big and powerful and amazing. God is what He says He is in Job 38-41.

CONCLUSION

Elisabeth Elliot knew her fair share of suffering. She lost her first husband, Jim Elliot, when he was killed by the Auca people after trying to reach them with the gospel. She remained single for thirteen years until she remarried. Her second husband died four years later. In her later years, she suffered the loss of her mind to the horrible disease we call dementia. With all the suffering in her life, she writes these beautiful and moving words, exactly in line with the book of Job: "God is God. If He is God, He is worthy of my worship and my service. I will find rest nowhere but in His will, and that will is infinitely, immeasurably, unspeakably beyond my largest notions of what He is up to."[73] That is the essence of what Job came to see. May that be the essence of what you and I come to see in our suffering.

---

73 Elisabeth Elliot, "Epilogue II," in *Through the Gates of Splendor* (Carol Stream: Tyndale, 1996), 267.

CHAPTER 11

EVIL AND SUFFERING

JOB 38:1-42:6

EVIL AND SUFFERING HAS PLAGUED and perplexed the human species since the beginning of time. After Adam and Eve sinned in the garden, all sorts of terrible evil and suffering entered the world: work is a four-letter word, childbirth is extremely painful, and relationships are a mess. Abortion, abuse, corruption, murder, rape, and war are only a few of the evils that plague our world.

For as long as people have been on the planet, we have tried to reconcile the fact of a good, wise, powerful, and just God with the evil that we see happening around us every day. Why would such a God allow suffering to exist in the world? Trying to reconcile these two things is technically called a theodicy. In layman's terms, we call this the "problem of evil."

The problem of evil is a problem for us in this chapter. Men and women throughout the ages, much smarter than me, have wrestled with this problem and given answers. I'm not proposing to scratch the surface on this topic here. We can't answer all the questions like, "Where did evil come from?" or "Did God create evil?" My intention is to show you how evil and suffering intersect in the book of Job. What does the book Job have to say about this topic? There are some things we can learn by looking at this book.

To recap, Job experienced devastating loss for no apparent reason. On the surface, it seems that God is unfair and unjust. At worst, He is cruel and evil to torture an innocent man. As the story of Job unfolds, Job and his four friends wrestle with the problem of evil. How can God be just and allow suffering to happen? After thirty-seven chapters, God finally speaks. He sets the record straight. With God's speech, we learn three wisdom lessons about evil and suffering. But before we get to these lessons, we need to deal with the mysterious creatures in chapters forty and forty-one.

THE IDENTITY OF BEHEMOTH AND LEVIATHAN

In chapters forty and forty-one, we are introduced to two creatures: Behemoth and Leviathan. The precise identity of these two creatures is debated. Among Bible-believing Christian theologians and pastors, some see these creatures as ordinary animals, like a hippopotamus and a crocodile or even a dinosaur and a dragon. Others see these creatures as symbols of evil and chaos in the world. Some say that Behemoth represents death and Leviathan represents Satan. It is beyond the purview of this book to go through all the arguments for each view.[74] Whatever

---

74   For a good presentation of the various views of these creatures, see: Ortlund, *Piercing Leviathan*, 119-144.

the precise identity of these creatures is, I do believe God is using them to speak about evil in the world.

Here are four quick reasons why I think these creatures represent evil in the world. First, outside the Bible, it was common in the time of Job, just as it is today, to have stories of dragons, beasts, and serpents that represent evil and chaos. Job would have understood what the Behemoth and Leviathan represented.[75] Think about your favorite fantasy novel, and the beasts that represent evil. Similar stories were told in Job's time. God used these stories Job was familiar with to communicate truth to him.

Second, inside the Bible, Behemoth is the Anglicized word of the Hebrew *behemah*. This word simply means "beasts." The Hebrew uses the plural form, which gives this word a sense of majesty. It is not describing one animal but describing a sort of "superbeast." This suggests a meaning more than a mere ordinary animal. This creature is something on another level, or at least represents something on another level. Leviathan is similar. The word is only mentioned four other times in Scripture. In each place it is used, it takes on the symbolism of supernatural evil (Job 3:8; Isa. 27:1; Ps. 74:14, 104:26).

Third, God moves in His first speech from natural creation and animals to the second speech about supernatural activity. This is why I think we get a different response from Job. Job responds to God's first speech with silence (Job 40:3-5). But Job responds

---

75 Ash, 419.

to the second speech with repentance (Job 42:1-6). His response is different because the Behemoth and Leviathan are on another plane. God, in essence, pulls back the curtain for Job to see in the second speech what he can't see with his natural eyes.[76]

Fourth, a hippo and crocodile don't completely fit the descriptions. Look at Job 40:24: "Can anyone capture [the Behemoth] when he is on watch, With barbs can anyone pierce *his* nose?" The problem is that, in the Ancient Near East, people were able to capture hippos. The Leviathan is said to omit fire and smoke. "Out of his mouth go burning torches; Sparks of fire leap forth. Out of his nostrils smoke goes forth as *from* a boiling pot and *burning* rushes" (Job 41:19-20). I don't know of any crocodiles that do that! Reading through these verses thoughtfully brings up similar questions about descriptions that do not add up to a hippo or a crocodile.

In summary, I believe these creatures are used as symbols of evil and the subsequent suffering that takes place in the world. I admit this is a tough case, but taking all the evidence together, I don't see how Behemoth and Leviathan are merely ordinary creatures. They may be some extinct creature. But even if they are, they are still pointing to a much deeper reality. It's not unlike other places in the Bible, like in the book of Revelation, when Satan is likened to a dragon and a serpent (Rev. 12:9, 20:2). Are dragons and serpents ordinary creatures? You tell me. The point is that Behemoth and Leviathan represent evil, suffering, and chaos in the world.

---

76   Ortlund, 151.

LESSON 1: EVIL AND SUFFERING HAVE A PLACE IN OUR WORLD

This is precisely what Job understood God to be saying. Job questioned God's justice; but God says that even though He is just, evil and suffering exist in our world. In fact, there exists greater evil and suffering than Job knew, until God revealed it to him. That's why God goes into so much detail about these two creatures with Job. God shows Job how much He knows about evil in the world, in all its detail; Job doesn't know the half of it! God reorients Job to reality because suffering caused Job to lose touch with reality. As we said in the last chapter, Job drew into himself. However, God says to him, "Job, your suffering is to be expected in a world full of evil."

I don't know about you; but when I look at my own heart and all the evil in the world, I can become so discouraged and depressed. Even with that, we also become so numb to the suffering happening all around us. We no longer receive our dose of evening news with Walter Cronkite; we now have accesses to the evil in the world 24/7 in our face on our phones. It's like God put a cell phone right up in Job's face. Job sees suffering and evil up close, but God doesn't stop there. There is a second lesson that He is communicating to Job which would start to bring hope.

LESSON 2: EVIL AND SUFFERING ARE LIMITED BY GOD

God does not want Job to only see the evil and affliction that exist in the world. He wants Job to see that He has limited the wickedness and suffering in the world.[77] God shows Job this over and over again, especially when He speaks of Leviathan. Let's start reading in Job 41:1-5:

> Can you draw out Leviathan with a fishhook? Or press down his tongue with a cord? Can you put a rope in his nose Or pierce his jaw with a hook? Will he make many supplications to you, Or will he speak to you soft words? Will he make a covenant with you? Will you take him for a servant forever? Will you play with him as with a bird, Or will you bind him for your maidens?

The implication is obvious: God is in control of the Leviathan. He limits its moves. How do you think this would have made Job feel? As Job is attacked by suffering on all sides, he feels alone and helpless. But once God reveals that evil is restrained, Job responds with awe and wonder. He says, "'I know that You can do all things, And that no purpose of Yours can be thwarted'" (Job 42:2). This is not a *general* confession of God's power. It is a *personal* confession from a man who was starting to see reality and the ways of God.

The other day, we were on a family walk in our neighborhood. As we approached one of the houses, I could see a large, evil-looking dog in the front yard—no fence, no leash. Of course, I was more concerned for my five-year-old's safety than my own. As we got closer and closer, the dog moved nearer to the sidewalk. I was bracing for a fight. And then we passed it. The dog didn't touch

---

77   Ash, 380.

us. The owners had an invisible fence. I was relieved. That's the way you're supposed to feel knowing that the evil and suffering, though painful and unwanted, has been placed in an invisible fence by God.

God limits heartache and pain in the world. No matter what suffering you're going through, you can know that it cannot escape God's control. In fact, God is limiting the affliction in your life. He is constantly restraining all the evil in the world. Yes, evil does exist. However, just like the Behemoth and the Leviathan, it is being restrained. And not only is it restrained, but a third lesson from these chapters also brings resolute hope.

LESSON 3: EVIL AND SUFFERING WILL BE DEFEATED AND DESTROYED

You see, if God has the power to limit evil and suffering in the world, He also has the power defeat and destroy it. We get glimpses of this with the Behemoth and Leviathan. To the Behemoth in Job 40:19, we see that that "[Behemoth] is the first of the ways of God; let his maker bring near his sword" to slay him. And to Leviathan in Job 41:7-8, He describes, "Can you fill his skin with harpoons, Or his head with fishing spears? Lay your hand on him; Remember the battle; you will not do it again!" These are just a few verses out of many where God says that He can and will defeat and destroy evil.

The natural question we ask is, "When will God defeat the Behemoth and Leviathan?" Perhaps this is what Job wanted to know. Thankfully, we have more revelation from God in His Word that satisfies. The greatest evil and suffering known to man was the killing of the innocent Son of God. But in this great evil came about the greatest good. It is in the cross that evil and its supernatural forces was ultimately defeated. The apostle Paul says, "When He had disarmed the rulers and authorities, He made a public display of them, having triumphed over them through [Christ]" (Col. 2:15). Evil and suffering is defeated with good—the goodness of the redemptive suffering on a cross.[78]

And because of the cross, one day, death, Satan, and sin will ultimately be destroyed; God will make all things new. Revelation 20:10 says that "the devil who deceived them was thrown into the lake of fire and brimstone, where the beast and the false prophet are also; and they will be tormented day and night forever and ever." And then we see in Revelation 21:1: "Then I saw a new heaven and a new earth; for the first heaven and the first earth passed away, and there is no longer *any* sea." All the evil and suffering that marks the present world will give way to a renewed world with no evil and suffering. Job didn't have this full revelation, but we do.

So let me summarize the essence of the message that God is communicating to us through the book of Job: evil and suffering have a place in our world, but He has placed limits on them. There is a coming day when He will defeat and destroy evil.

---

78   Ash, 422.

RESPONDING WITH REPENTANCE

So how should we respond to this word from God? What should our hearts do with the fact that suffering has a place in God's world, but God limits it until He one day defeats and destroys it?

Certainly, our response must parallel Job's. How did Job respond? Look at Job 42:6: "'Therefore I retract, And I repent in dust and ashes.'" The word *repent* used here has the sense of changing your mind about your circumstances so that you are comforted in them. This was true with Job. Finally, at the end of the book, he took comfort in God even as he experienced the dust and ashes of great suffering in his life. In other words, Job says that he turned to God even in his suffering. "Dust and ashes" represents a metaphor of suffering, not mourning. They represent all the loss that Job experienced. But in the end, he was finally able to see God—and, therefore, his suffering—clearly.

Two remarkable things are evident about Job's response. First, he repented—despite not being given a full explanation for his great suffering. However, Job is satisfied. For him, the "problem of evil" is finally put together in his mind: God is good, just, powerful, and wise; suffering exists in the world; and he is an innocent sufferer. All this can coexist at the same time. This knowledge is enough for Job. He sees God for Who He really is, and his heart is content without any specific reasons for why he had suffered.

The second remarkable thing about Job's response is that it occurs before he is restored at the end of the book (Job 42:10-17). As it turns out, Job really does worship God for God. In fact, the whole ordeal that Satan wanted to use to draw Job away from God in the beginning—by having Job suffer—this whole ordeal drew Job into a deeper relationship with God. Job now sees God like he never has before (Job 42:5).

In light of the evil and suffering in your life and in our world, right now in your heart, you can turn from yourself and your circumstances to the One Who allows a limited place for evil. Your suffering won't necessarily go away. But you can be satisfied, knowing that God has cleansed your evil heart in the cross of Christ. And that He will one day make all things new!

CONCLUSION

We should be thinking about this now, considering recent events. I write this on the heels of an eighteen-year-old gunman entering Robb Elementary School in Uvalde, Texas and killing nineteen children and two adults. It's heartbreaking. And it's a brutal reminder, as God told Job, that evil and suffering exist in our world. But Christianity never stops with despair and hopelessness. We know unspeakable pain and affliction exist in the world. We do not deny it. But we also know the God Who limits evil and suffering in the world. And we know the God Who will one day end all evil and suffering because of the work of Christ.

So we come to God in repentance once again, turning to Him as our only Source of hope and rescue from the Behemoth and Leviathan. He is the Hope that we have as believers. He is the Hope for our suffering world.

CHAPTER 12

THE GOSPEL AND SUFFERING

JOB 42:7-17

AS WE HAVE BEEN SUFFERING with Job, we have seen that this book certainly has much to say about a very relevant topic. We have learned many "wisdom lessons" as we have studied this book. As we wrap up the story of Job, I want to remind us that we cannot read and understand this book completely and fully until we see it in light of the gospel. We must see this story in light of Christ. Job 42 reveals a picture of the gospel. That is the main point of what I want to communicate in this final chapter. It is a picture of the gospel in two ways. First, the end of Job makes it clear this is a story of the gospel. Second, the main character is a type of Christ.

THE GOSPEL STORY IN THE BOOK OF JOB

The Lord offers these closing words in Job 42:7-9:

> It came about after the LORD had spoken these words
> to Job, that the LORD said to Eliphaz the Temanite,

"My wrath is kindled against you and against your two friends, because you have not spoken of Me what is right as My servant Job has. Now therefore, take for yourselves seven bulls and seven rams, and go to My servant Job, and offer up a burnt offering for yourselves, and My servant Job will pray for you. For I will accept him so that I may not do with you *according to your* folly, because you have not spoken of Me what is right, as My servant Job has." So Eliphaz the Temanite and Bildad the Shuhite *and* Zophar the Naamathite went and did as the LORD told them; and the LORD accepted Job.

This ending in the book of Job follows the gospel story. Humankind has sinned against God. God is angry at sin; He is jealous for His own glory. However, God doesn't deal with His people based on their sin but on the blood sacrifice and intercession of another. Let's break this down into a little more detail.

Humankind, which includes you and me, has sinned against God. In this story, it's the sin of the three friends. They haven't spoken rightly about God. Look at Job 42:7: "It came about after the LORD had spoken these words to Job, that the LORD said to Eliphaz the Temanite, 'My wrath is kindled against you and against your two friends, because you have not spoken of Me what is right as My servant Job has.'" We need to answer two questions about this statement. First, how did the friends speak wrong? Second, how did Job speak right?

First, we must address the speeches of Job's friends. They didn't necessarily have the wrong theology. What they said about God was right in a certain sense—He must be feared because of His manifold wisdom and great power. God also loves the righteous and hates sin. These three friends, in other words, could dot all their theological i's and cross all their theological t's. But when it came to *applying* their theology to Job, they were dead wrong.

It is not ultimately our theology that God cares about. Yes, we need to have correct theology. Yes, we need to have right thoughts of God. But if you don't apply your theology correctly, even to those who are suffering, you will "not speak of God what is right." You can say you believe in Christian love and unity all day long. But when you are hurt or offended, do you take the time to patiently, lovingly, and humbly listen to the person who you feel has wronged you? Do you ignore them, or do you go to them in love while thinking the best about them? How you apply your theology to others, or how you live your life, is ultimately an issue before God, not people. Sin is always vertical before it is horizontal. You will be held accountable to God for your words and actions.

Second, how did Job speak of God what was right? Certainly, in the beginning of the book, Job spoke right about God. He says some of the most beautiful words in the Scripture: "The LORD gave and the LORD has taken away. Blessed be the name of the LORD" (Job 1:21b). And yet, after the suffering would not abate, Job began to question God. Just like you and me, his suffering wore on him. Job lost touch with the truth because his suffering drew him inward to focus on himself. But interestingly, God doesn't call Job out for his words. From the Lord's perspective, overall, Job spoke of God what was right. However, he did lose touch with reality, and his relationship with God needed to be renewed.

Since humankind has sinned against their Creator, God is angry at sin. Job 42:7 says that God's "wrath is kindled" against Job's friends. God's anger and wrath is completely just and fair; for without anger toward sin, there would be no punishment of sin. And if there is no punishment of sin, God would not be just. God's anger is kindled against the friends for their words and actions.

Finally, not only has humankind sinned and deserves God's wrath, but God deals with His people in grace. Certainly, God did not have to show kindness toward Job's three friends. But God did show kindness by providing a blood sacrifice and a mediator for their sin. God's solution for their sin is found in Job 42:8a: "Now therefore, take for yourselves seven bulls and seven rams, and go to My servant Job, and offer up a burnt offering for yourselves, and My servant Job will pray for you."

What is interesting about this is that only one animal sacrifice would have been sufficient according to the law (Lev. 1:1-6:7). Yet God requires not one but fourteen animal sacrifices. It shows, again, the severity of the friend's words toward Job. Words matter. How you use all of your words—your spoken words or written words in various forms of texts, email, social media—matters to God. Job is requested to pray on behalf of his friends; he is taking on the role of a mediator. Job prays for them, "and the LORD accepted Job" (Job 42:9b). This truth and others point to Job as a type of Christ.

JOB IS A TYPE OF JESUS[79]

There are several ways in which Job is a type of Christ. Let me mention a few:

- Job, like Jesus, was an innocent sufferer. If there is any other likeness in the book of Job, this is one that certainly stands out. From the very beginning of the book of Job, even all throughout the book, even to the end, Job, though a sinner by nature, is an innocent sufferer (Job 1:1, 5, 8, 22; 2:3, 10; 1 Pet. 2:21-22).
- Job, like Jesus, was handed over to Satan to be inflicted with sufferings (Job 1:12, 2:6; Matt. 4:1; Acts 2:23).
- Job, like Jesus, was mocked and mistreated by his friends (Job 5:8; 11:12; Luke 22:54-62).
- Job, like Jesus, after his suffering, became a priestly mediator between God and man (Job 42:8; 1 Tim. 2:5; Heb. 7:25).

---

79   O'Donnell, 115.

- Job, like Jesus, became fully and publicly vindicated before God (Job 42:9; Acts 2:25-28).
- Job, like Jesus, in the end was exalted to receive honor and glory even more than before (Job 42:10-17; Eph. 1:19-23; Phil. 2:9-11).

It is crystal clear that Job is a type of Christ. We are meant to see Jesus in Job. It is not an accident. If the book of Job is a story of the gospel with a main character who is a type of Christ, what does this mean for us as believers living on the other side of the cross? Or to put the question differently, what does the gospel say about the suffering you and I experience? What are we supposed to see as Christians from the book of Job when we come to the end, where the loose pieces are tied together?

Really, there are two big picture lessons that we can take away, not only from this last section but from the entire book of Job. You could say they are summaries of the entire book, especially considering the end.

LESSON 1: THE GOSPEL CALLS YOU TO SUFFERING IN THIS LIFE

This is not a popular message today. It is not a popular message in any day. But the book of Job is not ultimately about suffering as a *human*. The book of Job is about suffering as a *believer*. As such, far from running from suffering, though it is hard and unwanted, you should embrace suffering as part of your call as a Christian. You are told over and over again that you will experience suffering as a believer (John 16:33; Rom. 8:35-39; 2 Tim. 3:12; 1 Pet. 4:12). The Bible reminds you often that you must take up your cross and follow Christ (Matt. 10:38, 16:24; Mark 8:34; Luke 9:23, 14:27). And you are even told that suffering is a gift from God: "For to you it has been granted for Christ's sake, not only to believe in Him, but also to suffer for His sake" (Phil. 1:29).

But you should not think the suffering envisioned here only applies to missionaries on the front lines. This gospel call to suffering applies to *all* Christians. The gospel call applies to all the suffering we face—physical, like cancer; financial, like job loss; emotional, like grief; or relational, like divorce. In other words, don't think the gospel call to suffering only applies to a man like Richard Wurmbrand, a man who suffered immensely for Christ. Yes, we honor men like him. Yes, we respect men like him. But the gospel call to suffering still applies to the ordinary suffering we face. Let me give you an example of a girl named Kelly. This is just part of her story.

Kelly was a young Christian when her accident happened. July 29, 2000, changed her life forever. "I was an active twelve-year old kid from Colorado," she says, "who loved theatre and snowboarding and couldn't wait to start seventh grade." She tells about a road trip with her family in which she was lying down in the back seat. Here's part of her story:

> Suddenly I woke up to the most horrifying sound
> of my brother screaming . . . I sat up just in time
> to see the guardrail in front of me, and then
> everything went black. I woke up to the sound of
> sirens, with the world spinning around me, and
> seven paramedics hovering two feet above my face.
> When they noticed I had regained consciousness,
> they shouted, "She's awake!" "Can you feel your
> toes? Can you feel your fingers? How many fingers
> am I holding up?" In utter confusion, I screamed,
> "I don't care about my toes! What happened? Who
> are you? Where is my family!?" After reconnecting
> with my family, my mom asked: "Can you feel your
> legs, honey?" I replied, "Yes, but Mom, where is my
> arm? Where is it? Is it attached?"

In the auto accident, Kelly suffered a severe arm injury that severed and snapped five key nerves from her spinal cord. One-fourth of her body was paralyzed. She suffers to this day, now over twenty years later, with chronic pain. And she has suffered multiple surgeries and financial debts because of the damage. Kelly, like Job, is a sufferer. Here's the point: her suffering is not outside the purview of the gospel call to suffer.[80] The point is that the gospel calls you to suffer, however ordinary your suffering may seem. Like Job, there may be no sin for why you are suffering. Simply, you have been called to suffer for His sake. But this isn't

---

80   John H. Walton, *Job: The NIV Application Commentary* (Grand Rapids: Zondervan, 2012), 87ff.

the final word for Christians. The book of Job continues, which is where we learn the second main lesson of the book.

LESSON 2: THE GOSPEL PROMISES YOU AN END TO SUFFERING IN THE LIFE TO COME

We love stories that end with "and they live happily ever after" because no one likes to read tragedy. (Sorry, Shakespeare!) Our world is broken. We know it. We feel it. But the gospel promises us that though we will not be delivered from all suffering in this life, we will be delivered from all suffering in the life to come.

The ending to the book of Job hints at this. It is quite interesting. Let's read it in Job 42:10-17:

> The LORD restored the fortunes of Job when he prayed for his friends, and the LORD increased all that Job had twofold. Then all his brothers and all his sisters and all who had known him before came to him, and they ate bread with him in his house; and they consoled him and comforted him for all the adversities that the LORD had brought on him. And each one gave him one piece of money, and each a ring of gold. The LORD blessed the latter *days* of Job more than his beginning; and he had 14,000 sheep and 6,000 camels and 1,000 yoke of oxen and 1,000 female donkeys. He had seven sons and three daughters. He named the first Jemimah, and the second Keziah, and the third Keren-happuch. In all the land no women were found so fair as Job's daughters; and their father gave them inheritance

> among their brothers. After this, Job lived 140 years,
> and saw his sons and his grandsons, four generations.
> And Job died, an old man and full of days.

The point is that Job has been restored. Now the question might be asked: is this a promise of twofold prosperity after suffering has ended? No, Job's situation was unique to him.

What the end of the book of Job teaches us is that God chose to bless Job not as a result of his behavior but as a result of God's grace. I say this because of what James says about Job in James 5:11: "We count those blessed who endured. You have heard of the endurance of Job and have seen the outcome of the Lord's dealings, that the Lord is full of compassion and is merciful." What I love about this passage is that is says Job endured, and God is gracious. It doesn't say God is gracious *because* Job endured. For it to be grace, it cannot be under any obligation. God did not have to bless Job in the end like He did. The book could have ended after Job 42:9. But we get a window into God's heart, which foreshadows what is to come.

When we look at this principle in the greater storyline of the Bible, we see that it is true that as Christians, we will be truly blessed in the life to come. Because God is "full of compassion and is merciful," one day we will be delivered from all suffering when God "will wipe away every tear from [our] eyes; and there will no longer be *any* death; there will no longer be *any mourning*, or crying, or pain; for the first things have passed away" (Rev. 21:4). The ending of the book of Job is a foreshadowing of the "happy ever after" for the believer in the end. For the Christian, suffering does not have the final word!

But this gospel promise that suffering will end in the life to come may seem so far away for some of you. You can hardly get by each day. You're in the thick of suffering, with no end in sight. So I want you to take to heart these words from James. Just before he references the endurance of Job and the compassion of God, James says in 5:7-8, "Therefore be patient, brethren, until the coming of the Lord . . . You too be patient [in your suffering]; strengthen your hearts, for the coming of the Lord is near." James and Job are saying that the gospel promises an end to suffering in the life to come. It is coming. Be patient!

CONCLUSION

As we press on, I don't know all the suffering in your life right now. I certainly don't know the suffering in your future. But Job is a book full of wisdom for suffering. In this way, Job, like all good books, is a timeless classic for the ages. I just feel bad for Job who had to go through it all to teach us these lessons! I know, however, Job would say it was worth it for all that his story teaches us. Let us not waste the lessons we've learned. Praise God for Job! Praise God for His grace in all our suffering!

> Oh, the depth of the riches both of the wisdom and knowledge of God! How unsearchable are His judgments and unfathomable His ways! For WHO HAS KNOWN THE MIND OF THE LORD, OR WHO

HAS BECOME HIS COUNSELOR? Or WHO HAS
FIRST GIVEN TO HIM THAT IT MIGHT BE PAID
BACK TO HIM AGAIN? For from Him and through
Him and to Him are all things. To Him *be* the glory
forever. Amen (Rom. 11:33-36).

APPENDIX

SUMMARY OF THE WISDOM LESSONS FOR A LIFE OF SUFFERING

1. Job 1:1-22 shows us that suffering happens to all people, even believers (Chapter 1).

2. Job 1:1-22 demonstrates how suffering arrives unexpectedly and fast (Chapter 1).

3. In Job 1:1-22, we see that suffering is an opportunity for us to trust God (Chapter 1).

4. Job 1:1-2:13 points out that God is Sovereign over all the suffering in our life (Chapter 2).

5. Job 1:1-2:13 shows us that Satan's accusations should lead us to examine our hearts (Chapter 3).

6. Job 1:1-2:13 reveals that Satan's accusations are ultimately accusations of God (Chapter 3).

7. Job 1:1-2:13 tell us that Satan's plans only go as far as God allows (Chapter 3).

8. Job 1:1-2:13 teaches us that Satan's accusations should lead us to Jesus (Chapter 3).

9. Job 2:11-3:26 points out how suffering produces feelings of loneliness (Chapter 4).

10. Job 2:11-3:26 demonstrates how one of the best ways to help someone suffering is to give the ministry of presence (Chapter 4).

11. Job 2:11-3:26 reveals that emotion is not in itself sinful (Chapter 4).

12. Job 2:11-3:26 points forward to how Jesus experienced loneliness and lament to deliver you from these emotions (Chapter 4).

13. Job 4:1-27:23 shows us that suffering is not necessarily the result of personal sin (Chapter 5).

14. Job 4:1-27:23 points out how grace reveals the greatest sufferer on the Cross (Chapter 5).

15. Job 4:1-27:23 remind us that in counseling a believer, we must remember that his or her suffering may not be the result of a specific sin (Chapter 6).

16. Job 4:1-27:23 reveal that in counseling a believer, we must remember that a Christian is simultaneously a saint, sinner, and a sufferer (Chapter 6).

17. Job 4:1-27:23 point to Jesus as the ultimate saint, "sinner," and sufferer (Chapter 6).

18. Job 28:1-28 tells us that wisdom in and for suffering is found in the fear of the Lord (Chapter 7).

19. Job 29:1-31:40 teaches us that in our suffering, we must look to Christ for our justification (Chapter 8).

20. Job 32:1-37:24 show how God does not owe us an explanation for our suffering (Chapter 9).

21. In Job 32:1-37:24, we see how God speaks in our suffering, if only we have ears to hear (Chapter 9).

22. Job 32:1-37:24 demonstrate that God is just in all the suffering in your life (Chapter 9).

23. Job 38:1-42:6 points out how suffering draws us into ourselves (Chapter 10).

24. Job 38:1-42:6 addresses how God is good–even in our suffering (Chapter 10).

25. Job 38:1:42:6 shows us that our fundamental need in our suffering is God (Chapter 10).

26. Job 38:1-42:6 acknowledges that evil and suffering have a place in our world (Chapter 11).

27. Job 38:1-42:6 tells us that evil and suffering are limited by God (Chapter 11).

28. Job 38:1-42:6 remind us that evil and suffering will be defeated and destroyed (Chapter 11).

29. Job 42:7-17 reveal that the gospel calls us to suffering in this life (Chapter 12).

30. In Job 42:7-17, we learn that the gospel promises us an end to suffering in the life to come (Chapter 12).

BIBLIOGRAPHY

Andersen, Francis. *Job: Tyndale Old Testament Commentaries*. Downers Grove: InterVarsity Press, 1976.

Ash, Christopher. *Job: The Wisdom of the Cross: Preach the Word*. Wheaton: Crossway, 2014.

Ash, Christopher. *Trusting God in the Darkness: A Guide to Understanding the Book of Job*. Wheaton: Crossway, 2021.

Beeke, Joel and Randall J. Pederson. *Meet the Puritans*. Grand Rapids: Reformation Heritage Books, 2006.

Beeke, Joel R. and Paul M. Smalley. *Reformed Systematic Theology, Vol 1, Revelation and God*. Wheaton: Crossway, 2019.

Belcher, Richard P. *Job: The Mystery of Suffering and God's Sovereignty: Focus on the Bible*. Scotland: Christian Focus, 2017.

Berg, Jim. *Created for His Glory: God's Purpose for Redeeming Your Life*. Greenville: Bob Jones University Press, 2002.

Bloom, Jon. *Don't Follow Your Heart: God's Ways Are Not Your Ways*. Minneapolis: Desiring God, 2015.

Elliot, Elisabeth. *Through the Gates of Splendor*. Carol Stream: Tyndale, 1996.

Emlet, Michael. *Cross Talk: Where Life & Scripture Meet*. Greensboro: New Growth Press, 2009. Kindle.

Emlet, Michael. *Saints, Sufferers, and Sinners: Loving Others as God Loves Us*. Greensboro: New Growth Press, 2020. Kindle.

Grudem, Wayne. *Systematic Theology*. Grand Rapids: Zondervan, 1994.

Jackson, David. *Crying out for Vindication: The Gospel According to Job*. Phillipsburg: P&R Publishing, 2007.

Jones, Hywel R. *Job*. Darlington: Evangelical Press, 2007.

Keller, Timothy. *Walking with God through Pain and Suffering*. New York: Penguin, 2013. Kindle.

Lewis, C.S. "The Problem of Pain," In *The Complete C. S. Lewis Signature Classics*. San Francisco: Harper One, 2002.

Luther, Martin. *Faith Alone: A Daily Devotional*. Edited by James C. Galvin. Grand Rapids: Zondervan, 2005. Kindle.

Mnookin, Seth. *The Panic Virus: The True Story Behind the Vaccine-Autism Controversy*. New York: Simon and Schuster, 2011.

O'Donnell, Douglas. *The Beginning and End of Wisdom: Preaching Christ from the First and Last Chapters of Proverbs, Ecclesiastes, and Job*. Wheaton: Crossway, 2011.

Ortlund, Dane. *Deeper: Real Change for Real Sinners*. Wheaton: Crossway, 2021. Kindle.

Ortlund, Eric. *Piercing Leviathan: God's Defeat of Evil in the Book of Job—New Studies in Biblical Theology*. Downers Grove: InterVarsity Press, 2021. Kindle.

Ortlund, Eric. *Suffering Wisely and Well: The Grief of Job and the Grace of God*. Wheaton: Crossway, 2022, 83-84.

Packer, J.I. *Knowing God*. Downers Grove: InterVarsity Press, 1973.

Piper, John. *God is the Gospel: Meditations of God's Love as the Gift of Himself*. Wheaton: Crossway, 2005.

Poythress, Vern. *Chance and the Sovereignty of God: A God-Centered Approach to Probability and Random Events*. Wheaton: Crossway, 2014.

Reinke, Tony. "The Secrets of God in Our Suffering: Trusting Him with Unanswered Questions." *Desiring God*. February 27,

2016. https://www.desiringgod.org/articles/the-secrets-of-god-in-our-suffering.

Risner, Vaneetha. "The Lord Gave and Took Away: Lessons on Suffering from Job." *Desiring God.* October 9, 2021. https://www.desiringgod.org/articles/the-lord-gave-and-took-away.

Selvaggio, Anthony. *Considering Job: Reconciling Sovereignty and Suffering.* Grand Rapids: Reformation Heritage Books.

Sproul, R.C. *Surprised by Suffering: The Role of Pain and Death in the Christian Life.* Orlando: Reformation Trust, 2009. Kindle.

Tchividjian, Tullian. *Glorious Ruin: How Suffering Sets You Free.* Colorado Springs: David Cook, 2012. Kindle.

Tripp, Paul. *A Quest for Something More: Living for Something Bigger Than You.* Greensboro: New Growth Press, 2008.

Tripp, Paul. *Instruments in the Redeemer's Hands: People in Need of Change Helping People in Need of Change.* Phillipsburg: P&R Publishing, 2002.

Tripp, Paul. *Suffering: Gospel Hope When Life Doesn't Make Sense.* Wheaton: Crossway Publishing, 2018.

Tripp, Paul. *Whiter Than Snow: Meditations on Sin and Mercy.* Wheaton: Crossway Publishing, 2008.

Walton, John. *Job: The NIV Application Commentary.* Grand Rapids: Zondervan Publishing, 2012.

Welch, Edward. *When People are Big and God is Small: Overcoming Peer Pressure, Codependency, and the Fear of Man.* Phillipsburg: P&R Publishing, 1997.

ABOUT THE AUTHOR

DANIEL W. BURRUS (M.A., THM) is a teacher with Equipping Leaders International, a ministry that equips under-resourced leaders around the world. He, along with his wife and four children, currently reside in Cedar Rapids, Iowa.

INDEX

Exodus 33:18 115

Leviticus 1:1-6:7 132

Job 1:1 6, 133

Job 1:1-2:13 15, 27

Job 1:2-3 7

Job 1:5 6, 133

Job 1:6-12 9, 28

Job 1:7a 17

Job 1:8 17, 81, 88, 133

Job 1:12 17, 36, 133

Job 1:13-19 8

Job 1:14-15 9

Job 1:15a 16

Job 1:16 9, 16

Job 1:17 16

Job 1:18-19 16

Job 1:20 43, 81

Job 1:20-21 11

Job 1:21 18, 80, 81

Job 1:21b 12, 131

Job 1:22 6, 43, 53, 133

Job 2:1-6 9

Job 2:1-8 29

Job 2:2 17

Job 2:3 17, 133

Job 2:6 17, 36, 133

Job 2:7 17, 59

Job 2:10 18, 21, 53, 133

Job 2:11-3:26 37

Job 2:11-13 39

Job 2:13 40, 41

Job 3:1 43

Job 3:3-10 42, 43

Job 3:8 121

Job 3:11-19 43

Job 3:20-26 43

Job 4 49, 59

Job 4:2-5 61

Job 4:7 51
Job 4:8 56
Job 5:6 56
Job 5:8 62, 133
Job 5:8-9 51
Job 5:17 52
Job 7:4 45
Job 7:13-14 45
Job 7:19 24
Job 8:5-6 60
Job 9:21-22 61
Job 11:12 133
Job 13:25 37
Job 13:28 37
Job 16:1-2 60
Job 16:6 61
Job 16:16 45
Job 18 84
Job 19 39
Job 19:13-19 38
Job 19:17 45
Job 19:20 45
Job 21:6 45
Job 23:3 98
Job 23:8-9 98
Job 27 51

Job 28 72
Job 28:1-11 73
Job 28:1-28 71
Job 28:12 72
Job 28:15-19 74
Job 28:23 74
Job 28:28 2, 74
Job 28-31 51
Job 29 39, 84
Job 29:1-31:40 83
Job 29:2-6 38
Job 29:7-20 85
Job 30 86
Job 30:17 45
Job 30:24-25 86
Job 30:27 45
Job 30:30 45
Job 31:1-4 87
Job 31:5-8 87
Job 31:9-12 87
Job 31:13-15 87
Job 31:16-23 87
Job 31:24-25 87
Job 31:26-28 87
Job 31:29-30 87
Job 31:31-32 87

Job 31:33-34 87

Job 31:35-37 88

Job 31:38-40 87

Job 32 51

Job 32:1-37:24 95

Job 32:2-5 97

Job 33:12-13 98

Job 33:14 100

Job 33:15-16 100

Job 33:19 100

Job 33:23-24 100

Job 34:5-6 99

Job 34:12 99

Job 35:2 103

Job 37:23 104

Job 38:1 107

Job 38:1-42:6 107, 119

Job 38:25-27 112

Job 38:31-33 109

Job 38:39-41 112

Job 38-41 116

Job 39:13-18 110

Job 39:14 110

Job 39:15 110

Job 39:16 110

Job 39:17 110

Job 40:3-5 111, 121

Job 40:4 111

Job 40:6-8 112

Job 40:19 125

Job 40:24 122

Job 41:1-5 124

Job 41:7-8 125

Job 41:19-20 122

Job 42 129

Job 42:1-6 121

Job 42:2 124

Job 42:3b 111

Job 42:5 114, 128

Job 42:6 127

Job 42:7 88, 130, 132

Job 42:7-8 43

Job 42:7-9 129

Job 42:7-17 129

Job 42:8 133

Job 42:8a 132

Job 42:9 133, 138

Job 42:9b 132

Job 42:10-17 127, 133, 137

Psalm 19:7 79

Psalm 62:8 44

Psalm 74:14 121

Psalm 104:26 121

Psalm 119:98 80

Proverbs 11:2 78

Ecclesiastes 3:4 46

Isaiah 27:1 121

Isaiah 52-53 69

Isaiah 55:8-9 103

Jeremiah 2:13 116

Matthew 1:22-23 41

Matthew 3:17 68

Matthew 4:1 133

Matthew 10:38 134

Matthew 16:16 68

Matthew 16:24 134

Matthew 17:5 68

Matthew 26:36-46 46

Matthew 27:46 46 100

Matthew 28:20 3

Mark 8:34 134

Luke 9:23 134

Luke 14:27 134

Luke 22:31 36

Luke 22:32 36

Luke 22:54-62 133

John 1:14 41

John 9:1-3 53

John 11:35 46

John 16:33 134

Acts 2:23 133

Acts 2:25-28 133

Romans 1:4 68

Romans 3:26 104

Romans 5:1 92

Romans 5:1-2 92

Romans 6:6-7 63

Romans 6:6-8 63

Romans 6-8 63

Romans 7:18-19 63

Romans 8:1 36

Romans 8:18 63

Romans 8:22 63

Romans 8:28 23

Romans 8:32 23

Romans 8:35 23

Romans 8:35-39 134

Romans 11:33-36 139

Romans 12:15 41

1 Corinthians 1:30 80

1 Corinthians 3:16 41

1 Corinthians 6:19 41

2 Corinthians 1:4 101

2 Corinthians 5:21 68

2 Corinthians 6:16 41

Galatians 3:13 69

Galatians 6:7 56

Ephesians 1:19-23 133

Ephesians 4:11-12 101

Ephesians 4:15 101

Philippians 1:29 134

Philippians 2:7 69

Philippians 2:9-11 133

Philippians 3:10 115

Colossians 2:3 80

Colossians 2:15 126

Colossians 3:16 101

1 Timothy 2:5 133

2 Timothy 1:14 41

2 Timothy 3:12 134

2 Timothy 3:16 1

Hebrews 1:1-2a 101

Hebrews 4:15 47, 68

Hebrews 5:8 69

Hebrews 7:25 133

Hebrews 11:1-2 91

Hebrews 12:5 52

Hebrews 13:5 47

James 1:2 80

James 1:5 80

James 5:7-8 138

James 5:11 iii, 137

1 Peter 1:20 104

1 Peter 2:21-22 133

1 Peter 2:22-23 104

1 Peter 2:23 104

1 Peter 4:12 134

1 Peter 5:8 36

1 John 3:2 116

Revelation 7:17 47

Revelation 12:9 122

Revelation 12:10 31

Revelation 20:2 122

Revelation 20:10 126

Revelation 21:1 126

Revelation 21:4 138

MORE FROM AMBASSADOR INTERNATIONAL

Like a chef who seasons the meal in such a way that the distinctive flavors of each element is enhanced, Brian Onken invites readers of *More Than a Clever Story* into an invigorating and fresh taste of what Jesus says in His parables. Reading each parable attentive to Jesus' own words and the context in which these stories are found, you'll hear the voice of the Savior in renewed ways. No longer will you think of His parables as clever stories, but you'll find them to be life-giving words from Jesus.

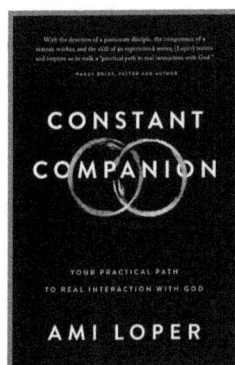

Every human heart longs to be truly known and deeply loved. Each person has a God-given longing for fulfillment and a sense of belonging that is met only in a relationship with God. But does God really want a relationship with you? Yes, and He demonstrates His desire for that over and over again in Scripture. *Constant Companion* shows readers how to get past feelings of unworthiness, unwillingness, and other distractions and how to listen to God's voice through the practices of meditation, prayer, and Scripture-reading.

Most of us know Who Jesus is and would admit He was a good and kind Teacher while here on earth. But He is so much more—He is our Savior and God and worthy of all our worship. Through an in-depth study into the book of Hebrews, Joshua West and Gary Wilkerson take apart each verse, drawing the reader to a closer look at the Man Who lived here on earth for a short time and then became our Sacrifice to save us from our sins and live with us eternally in Heaven with Him. If you are searching for something more from God, dive into this study and drink in the jaw-dropping beauty of our Jesus.